RAINBOW BAKES
40 SHOW-STOPPING SWEET TREATS

Mima Sinclair

Photography by Danielle Wood

Mima Sinclair is a food writer who has cooked, tested, written and developed recipes for numerous cookbooks, food magazines and worked with a number of top chefs. This is her third book with Kyle Books, following the bestselling **Mug Cakes** and **Gingerbread Wonderland**, which have sold over half a million copies worldwide!

KYLE BOOKS

For my sisters Linsey, Storm, Amber and Sarah.

When you unleash a child in the kitchen with food colouring, a bake just isn't as gratifying without it. To this day I still can't understand why Dad turned down slices of our psychedelic rainbow masterpieces!

First published in Great Britain in 2016 by
Kyle Books, an imprint of Kyle Cathie Ltd
192-198 Vauxhall Bridge Road
London SW1V 1DX
general.enquiries@kylebooks.com
www.kylebooks.co.uk

10 9 8 7 6 5 4 3 2 1

ISBN 978 0 85783 389 1

Designer: Louise Leffler
Photographer: Danielle Wood
Illustrator: Sarah Leuzzi
Food Stylist: Mima Sinclair
Props Stylist: Lauren Miller and Lydia Brun
Project Editor: Sophie Allen
Editorial Assistant: Hannah Coughlin
Production: Nic Jones, Gemma John and
Lisa Pinnell

A Cataloguing in Publication record for this title
is available from the British Library.

Colour reproduction by ALTA London
Printed in Slovenia
International Printing Ltd.

CONTENTS

INTRODUCTION

You know how you have always been told not to play with your food? Well forget it all! I give you permission to paint your kitchen and your food with the colours of the rainbow.

Adding a little colour pop to your bakes is a fantastic way to show personality and style in the most delicious way possible. Whether you want jaws to drop when your cake is revealed, to hear a chorus of 'ooh' when you slice into it, or to be asked 'how did you do that!?' Now is the time to get colour obsessed – I promise you tea time will never be the same again.

Vibrant and playful recipes have become so popular in recent years that since the explosion of the first rainbow cake it seems we can't get enough of eye-popping layered bakes, brightly swirled bagels and even rainbow cheese toasties! When people see their first rainbow cake it mentally goes down on their baking bucket list! And I have a few more to add to your must bake-and-devour list, so whether you're after a tiny rainbow treat or an indulgent six-layered extravaganza, you've come to the right place.

Baking can be a lot of fun and experimenting in the kitchen can lead to incredible creations to show off to friends and family. What isn't so fun is when it goes wrong and you can't work out why. The two common factors which can cause a rainbow meltdown are food colouring and sprinkles, but fear not I've included some great tips to make sure your rainbows come out perfectly.

So what are you waiting for? Taste the rainbow today!

TIPS & TECHNIQUES

RAINBOW SPRINKLES

There are so many different rainbow sprinkles available the main problem is trying not to buy all of them!

Nonpareils/hundreds and thousands – tiny spherical balls
Jumbo sprinkles – a larger version of nonpareils
Vermicelli/strands – small strands
Jimmies – a large thicker version of vermicelli
Confetti – small flat round discs

SPRINKLES FOR DECORATING

You can use whatever takes your fancy! There are no rules here, just have fun.

SPRINKLES FOR BAKING

Before you embark on a funfetti baking extravaganza please take note. It might seem like a simple task – just fold through some rainbow sprinkles and voilà! However, not all rainbow sprinkles can withstand the baking process.

Firstly, the best and brightest results come from artificially coloured sprinkles, their naturally coloured sprinkle counterparts struggle to be bright enough and loose their colour while baking.

Secondly, you must use nice big, fat rainbow sprinkles, also known as jimmies or confetti sprinkles. Buy the most vibrant colour selection you can find as they will produce the most impressive of rainbow flecks in your bakes. Any kind of nonpareils tend to be too small and the colour will be lost long before the bake is out of the oven.

FOOD COLOURING

Liquid food colouring used to be the only choice available but now we are spoilt for choice with pastes, gels and powdered versions. However, these can all create dramatically different outcomes. I like to use gels and pastes, because they produce vibrant colours and you only require a small amount. Good brands to look out for are Wilton, Sugarflair and Americolor. I find that some of the liquid colourings can require a large volume to reach my desired shade and therefore can upset the liquid content of my bake. They can also have an odd flavour which lingers even after baking.

LIQUID

These water-based dyes are readily available in the baking aisle of almost all supermarkets. They tend to come in little bottles which allow you to drip the dye, drop by drop, into your mixture. They are the least intense so can be good for pastel shades, but when you require a bolder tone these dyes can let you down. You can end up using a significant amount to try to achieve your desired colour, so much so the extra liquid can upset the ingredient ratios.

Good for – icing & pastel sponge

GEL

These thick gel-type liquids are available in the baking aisle of large supermarkets, cook shops or online. They typically come in small squeezy bottles that allow you to drop a drip at a time into your mixture. The colour is more concentrated than the liquid colouring so a smaller amount will impart a more vivid colour, great when you want to minimize the amount of liquid added.

Good for – icing, sponge & dough

PASTE

A very thick, super concentrated version of a gel colour, these are available in cook stores and online. These pastes come in little pots and you can dip a toothpick or knife tip in to scoop out the tiniest bit of paste. A very small amount will produce a lovely intense, saturated colour. Great for recipes where minimal liquid is desired. These pastes do, however, require more mixing to blend the colour to avoid a marbled, uneven effect, which can cause over-mixing in certain recipes i.e. biscuits and doughs.

Good for – confectionary, icing & sponge

POWDER

A powder form of food dye. Trickier to get hold of but available in some cook shops and online. It comes in small pots and this dry mix is ideal for colouring when no moisture is desired. It can be difficult to combine into thick doughs or batters but very successful for colouring bakes where sensitivity to liquid is high.

Good for – macaroons & meringues

NATURAL FOOD COLOURING

A water-based colour derived from natural and plant sources i.e. turmeric and beetroot. They come in little bottles which allow you to drip the dye, drop by drop, into your mixture. These are healthier than the synthetic colourings. Available in health food stores they will achieve muted shades, but will struggle with the vibrant tones required to make rainbow layer cake.

Good for – allergy sufferers

WHOLE CAKES

RAINBOW CAKE

SERVES 18   PREP TIME: 1½ HOURS, PLUS COOLING, CHILLING AND SETTING   COOK TIME: 40–50 MINUTES

There is nothing quite as spectacular as a classic rainbow cake.

750g unsalted butter, softened,
  plus extra for greasing
750g caster sugar
9 large eggs, lightly beaten
750g self-raising flour, sifted
1 teaspoon fine salt
100ml whole milk
2 teaspoons vanilla extract
food colouring pastes (purple, blue,
  green, yellow, orange and pink)

FOR THE CREAM CHEESE ICING

800g unsalted butter, softened
1kg icing sugar, sifted
800g full-fat cream cheese
1 teaspoon vanilla extract

TO DECORATE

25g rainbow confetti sprinkles
2 candy necklaces
2 wooden skewers

MAKE EDIBLE BUNTING TO DECORATE YOUR CAKE BY TYING CANDY NECKLACE TO SKEWERS.

1. Preheat the oven to 180°C/gas mark 4. Grease and line 3 x 20cm round cake tins with baking parchment.

2. Using an electric hand whisk, beat the butter and caster sugar together in a large bowl until light and fluffy. Gradually add the eggs, beating well after each addition. Sift in the flour and salt and fold through evenly with a large spoon. Stir in the milk and vanilla extract until combined.

3. Weigh the mixture, divide it between six bowls. Add a different food colouring paste to each bowl, until you reach your required colours. Spoon three of the cake mixtures into the tins, spreading evenly. Bake for 20–25 minutes, or until a skewer inserted into the centre comes out clean. Leave to cool for 5 minutes, then turn out onto a wire rack and leave to cool completely. Wash and dry, then re-grease and line the cake tins. Bake the remaining coloured cake mixtures and cool as before.

4. Once the cake layers are cold, use a serrated knife to trim the tops to make the cakes level, then trim the cake edges (using an upturned plate that is just smaller than the cake, as a guide).

5. For the cream cheese icing, beat the butter and icing sugar together in a bowl until light and fluffy. Gradually beat in the cream cheese, a spoonful at a time, then beat in the vanilla extract until smooth and combined. Sandwich the cake layers together, spreading a few tablespoons of the icing between each layer, starting with the purple sponge, then the blue, green, yellow, orange and pink ones. Cover the cake completely with a thin layer of icing to catch all the crumbs, then chill in the fridge for 1 hour.

6. Thickly spread the remaining icing over the cake to cover it, then use a palette knife or icing scraper to create a lovely flat top and sides. Stick rainbow confetti to the bottom half of the cake, tapering them off as you go up. Leave to set in the fridge for 1 hour, then remove the cake 20 minutes before serving.

PIÑATA CAKE

SERVES 18   PREP TIME: 1¼ HOURS, PLUS COOLING   COOK TIME: 20-25 MINUTES

The ultimate party centrepiece – one slice of this impressive cake will reveal its hidden sweet secret! Choose your own colour icing and type of sweets.

350g unsalted butter, softened,
    plus extra for greasing
350g caster sugar
6 large eggs
350g plain flour
2½ teaspoons baking powder
1 teaspoon fine salt
1 teaspoon vanilla extract
4 tablespoons whole milk

FOR THE BUTTERCREAM

500g unsalted butter, softened
1kg icing sugar, sifted
1 teaspoon vanilla extract
pink food colouring paste
    (or your chosen colour)

TO DECORATE

1kg colourful mixed sweets

YOU WILL NEED

round cookie cutter, about
    10cm diameter

1. Preheat the oven to 180°C/gas mark 4. Grease and line 3 x 20cm round cake tins with baking parchment.

2. Using an electric hand whisk, beat the butter and caster sugar together in a large bowl until light and fluffy. Add the eggs, one at a time, beating well after each addition. Sift in the flour, baking powder and salt and fold through evenly with a large spoon. Stir in the vanilla extract and milk until combined.

3. Divide the mixture between the prepared tins, spreading evenly. Bake for 20-25 minutes, or until a skewer inserted into the centre comes out clean. Leave to cool in the tins for 5 minutes, then turn out onto a wire rack and leave to cool completely.

4. Meanwhile, for the buttercream, beat the butter, icing sugar and vanilla extract together in a bowl until light and fluffy. Stir in pink food colouring paste, until you reach your required colour.

5. Once the cake layers are cold, take one layer and cut a hole out of the centre using the cookie cutter. Repeat with a second cake layer. Sandwich these two layers together with some pink buttercream, then cover the top layer with more buttercream. Fill the central hole with mixed sweets, then place the final uncut cake sponge on top to enclose the sweets completely.

6. Use the remaining buttercream to cover the cake completely, then gradually (without eating too many!) cover the whole cake with the remaining mixed sweets.

HIDDEN CENTRE LOAF CAKE

SERVES 10   PREP TIME: 1¼ HOURS, PLUS COOLING, FREEZING AND SETTING   COOK TIME: 2 HOURS 20 MINUTES

The gorgeous paint-like dribbles on this cake will have people squealing! But just wait until you slice it open to reveal a hidden rainbow number running through its centre.

FOR THE HIDDEN NUMBER CUT-OUTS
200g unsalted butter, softened, plus extra for greasing
200g caster sugar
3 large eggs
200g self-raising flour
¼ teaspoon fine salt
1 teaspoon vanilla extract
3 tablespoons whole milk
food colouring pastes (purple, blue, green, orange and pink)

FOR THE VANILLA SPONGE
330g unsalted butter, softened
330g caster sugar
5 large eggs
330g self-raising flour
½ teaspoon fine salt
1 teaspoon vanilla extract
5 tablespoons whole milk

FOR THE DRIBBLE ICING
200g royal icing sugar, sifted
food colouring pastes (blue, green, yellow, orange and pink)

YOU WILL NEED
6 disposable piping bags (including 1 large one)
cookie cutter number or shape, about 5 x 6cm

1. Preheat the oven to 180°C/gas mark 4. Grease and line an 18 x 12 x 7cm loaf tin with baking parchment.

2. For the hidden number cut-outs, using an electric hand whisk, beat the butter and caster sugar together in a large bowl until light and fluffy. Add the eggs, one at a time, beating well after each addition. Sift in the flour and salt and fold through evenly with a large spoon. Stir in the vanilla extract and milk until combined.

3. Divide the mixture between five bowls and stir a little food colouring paste into each portion, then spoon each into a separate piping bag and snip a ½cm hole off the tips. Pipe the coloured cake mixtures into the prepared loaf tin, alternating the colours as you go to create a crazy marbled effect. Tap the tin on the surface to remove any air bubbles.

4. Bake for 1 hour–1 hour 10 minutes, or until a skewer inserted into the centre comes out clean. Leave to cool in the tin for 10 minutes, then turn out onto a wire rack and leave to cool completely.

5. Cut the cold loaf cake into 2.5cm-thick slices. Use your chosen cutter to cut out the number or shape from each slice, then lay the cut-outs on a baking tray. Place the tray in the freezer for 15 minutes while you make the vanilla sponge. Save the cake scraps for making cake pops.

6. Preheat the oven again to 180°C/gas mark 4. Wash and dry, then re-grease and line the loaf tin. Make the vanilla sponge mixture following the instructions given above in step 2. Pour 2cm of the cake mixture into the base of the prepared loaf

tin, then spoon the remaining mixture into the large piping bag and snip a 2cm hole off the tip.

7. Position the frozen cake cut-outs upright (and close together) in a single row down the centre of the tin. Mark the front of your tin with a piece of tape if you are using a number cut-out (so you cut the correct end to reveal forward-facing numbers, for serving). Pipe the remaining vanilla cake mixture around the cut-outs and all over the top to cover them completely, ensuring you fill in any small holes. Smooth the top with the back of a spoon.

8. Bake for 1 hour–1 hour 10 minutes as above, then turn out and cool as before. Keep track of the marked end of the cake, so you know which end of the cake to slice into to have the forward-facing numbers.

9. For the icing, place the icing sugar in a bowl and add 2 teaspoons of cold water. Stir until smooth, then add a little extra water until you have a thick but just runny icing. Divide between five small bowls and stir a little food colouring paste into each portion.

10. Once the cake is cold, spoon alternate blobs of icing onto the top of the cake, encouraging them to dribble down the sides. If your icing is too thick, add a drop more water; if it is too runny, add a spoonful of extra icing sugar.

11. Leave to set at room temperature for 4 hours before slicing and serving.

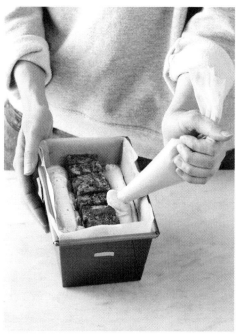

FUNFETTI CAKE

SERVES 16   PREP TIME: 50 MINUTES, PLUS COOLING AND CHILLING   COOK TIME: 20 MINUTES

What is the secret to a successful funfetti cake? Big, fat rainbow sprinkles, that's what! Their smaller brothers and sisters simply won't do the job.

250g unsalted butter, softened,
plus extra for greasing
250g caster sugar
4 large eggs
250g plain flour
2 teaspoons baking powder
1 teaspoon fine salt
1 teaspoon vanilla extract
3 tablespoons whole milk
100g rainbow jimmies (a large
thicker version of vermicelli)
– I use Wilton's

FOR THE BUTTERCREAM

400g unsalted butter, softened
800g icing sugar, sifted
1 teaspoon vanilla extract

TO DECORATE

300g rainbow sprinkles (nonpareils/
hundreds and thousands)

1. Preheat the oven to 180°C/gas mark 4. Grease and line 3 x 18cm round cake tins with baking parchment.

2. Using an electric hand whisk, beat the butter and caster sugar together in a large bowl until light and fluffy. Add the eggs, one at a time, beating well after each addition. Sift in the flour, baking powder and salt and fold through evenly with a large spoon. Stir in the vanilla extract and milk until combined, then fold in the sprinkles until evenly dispersed.

3. Divide the mixture between the prepared tins, spreading evenly. Bake for 20 minutes, or until a skewer inserted into the centre comes out clean. Leave to cool in the tins for 5 minutes, then turn out onto a wire rack and leave to cool completely.

4. Meanwhile, for the buttercream, beat the butter, icing sugar and vanilla extract together in a bowl until light and fluffy. Once the cake layers are cold, sandwich them together with some of the buttercream, then coat the cake completely with the remaining buttercream. Chill in the fridge for 1 hour.

5. To decorate, pour the rainbow sprinkles into a large baking tray. Carefully lift the cake and roll it through the sprinkles, pressing them into the buttercream and using your hands to gently press them into the top of the cake. Slice and serve.

NAKED RAINBOW TIER

SERVES 16   PREP TIME: 40 MINUTES, PLUS COOKING   COOK TIME: 20-25 MINUTES

After baking a rainbow, a naked cake is the perfect way to show it off.

165g unsalted butter, softened,
plus extra for greasing
400g caster sugar
5 large egg whites
1½ teaspoons vanilla extract
115g soured cream
375g plain flour
1 tablespoon baking powder
1 teaspoon bicarbonate of soda
½ teaspoon fine salt
240ml whole milk
food colouring pastes (purple, blue,
green, yellow, orange and red)

FOR THE CREAM CHEESE ICING

250g unsalted butter, softened
350g icing sugar, sifted
250g full-fat cream cheese
1 teaspoon vanilla extract

YOU WILL NEED

1 disposable piping bag

CREATING A TIERED EFFECT CAN BE A SIMPLE BUT VISUALLY EXCITING WAY TO LAYER YOUR CAKE

1. Preheat the oven to 180°C/gas 4. Grease and line 3 x 20cm cake tins and 3 x 18cm cake tins with baking parchment.

2. Using an electric hand whisk, beat the butter and caster sugar together in a large bowl until light and fluffy. Add the egg whites, one at a time, beating well after each addition. Lightly beat in the vanilla extract and soured cream. Sift the flour, baking powder, bicarbonate of soda and salt into a bowl, then add to the egg white mixture in three batches, alternating with the milk. Fold through evenly with a large spoon.

3. Divide the mixture between six smaller bowls. Take a rounded tablespoon out of three of the bowls and add one to each of the other bowls. Add a little purple, blue and green food colouring paste to the fuller bowls and yellow, orange and red colouring paste to the smaller bowls, mixing until combined.

4. Spoon the purple, blue and green mixtures into the 20cm cake tins, spreading evenly. Bake for 10-12 minutes, or until a skewer inserted into the centre comes out clean. Leave to cool for 5 minutes, then turn out onto a wire rack and leave to cool.

5. Spoon the yellow, orange and red mixtures into the prepared 18cm cake tins, spreading evenly, then bake and cool as above.

6. Once the cake layers are cold, using a serrated knife, carefully trim the crusts off the edges of the cakes. Use the base of a slightly smaller cake tin or an upturned plate to cut around.

7. For the icing, beat the butter and icing sugar together in a bowl until light and fluffy. Gradually beat in the cream cheese, a spoonful at a time, then beat in the vanilla extract until smooth. Spoon one-third of the icing into the piping bag, then snip a 1½ cm hole off the tip. Pipe a circle of icing around the inner edge of the purple sponge, then fill the centre in with a few tablespoons of icing and spread out evenly. Top with the blue sponge and then repeat the icing steps with the remaining icing, leaving the top of the cake un-iced.

ANTI-GRAVITY CAKE

SERVES 18   PREP TIME: 1½ HOURS, PLUS COOLING, SETTING AND CHILLING   COOK TIME: 20-25 MINUTES

Watch kids and adults have their minds blown with this edible illusion –
the anti-gravity cake, which is great for themed party centrepieces!

350g unsalted butter, softened,
   plus extra for greasing
350g caster sugar
6 large eggs
350g plain flour
2½ teaspoons baking powder
1 teaspoon fine salt
1 teaspoon vanilla extract
4 tablespoons whole milk

FOR THE BUTTERCREAM

500g unsalted butter, softened
1kg icing sugar, sifted
2 teaspoons vanilla extract
food colouring (pink and blue)

FOR THE DRIBBLE ICING

100g royal icing sugar, sifted
food colouring pastes (yellow
   and purple)

TO DECORATE

30g white chocolate (minimum
   30% cocoa solids), melted
100g rainbow sprinkles
unicorn (optional)

YOU WILL NEED

small paintbrush
1 thick wooden skewer
piping bag fitted with a large closed
   star nozzle
small clear plastic pot

1. Preheat the oven to 180°C/gas mark 4. Grease and line 3 x 20cm round cake tins with baking parchment.

2. Using an electric hand whisk, beat the butter and caster sugar together in a large bowl until light and fluffy. Add the eggs, one at a time, beating well after each addition. Sift in the flour, baking powder and salt and fold through evenly with a large spoon. Stir in the vanilla extract and milk until combined.

3. Divide the mixture between the prepared tins, spreading evenly. Bake for 20–25 minutes, or until a skewer inserted into the centre comes out clean. Leave to cool in the tins for 5 minutes, then turn out onto a wire rack and leave to cool completely.

4. Meanwhile, for the buttercream, beat the butter, icing sugar and vanilla extract together in a bowl until light and fluffy. Spoon a sixth of the buttercream into a separate bowl, then stir in a little pink food colouring paste and set aside. Add blue food colouring paste to the remaining buttercream.

5. Once cold, cut each sponge cake in half horizontally. Sandwich the cake layers together with some of the blue buttercream and then coat the cake completely with the remainder.

6. For the dribble icing, place the icing sugar in a bowl and add 2 teaspoons of cold water. Stir until smooth, then add a little extra water until you have a thick but just runny icing. Divide between two small bowls and stir a little yellow food colouring paste into one portion and purple into the other.

7. Spoon a trail of yellow icing around the top edge of the cake, encouraging a little dribble down the sides. Leave for 30 minutes to set, then repeat with the purple icing. Leave for a further 30 minutes to set.

ONCE YOU MASTER THE TECHNIQUE, YOU CAN SUSPEND ALL YOUR FAVOURITE TREATS ABOVE THE CAKE!

8. Meanwhile, for the decoration, using a small paintbrush, brush two-thirds of a thick wooden skewer in the melted white chocolate, then coat in rainbow sprinkles. Place in the fridge to set hard.

9. Once the dribble icing has set, spoon the pink buttercream into the piping bag, then pipe small stars around the top edge of the cake. Take your sprinkle-coated skewer and insert into the centre of the cake, pushing it in at an angle until the uncovered wooden end is no longer visible (just the sprinkle-coated part is visible). Pour a pile of the rainbow sprinkles around the base of the skewer and press them in lightly.

10. Put the remaining rainbow sprinkles into the small clear pot and cover the top neatly with clingfilm to stop all the sprinkles from falling out. Carefully pierce one corner of the pot, then carefully insert the top end of the sprinkle-coated skewer into it, so it hooks into the neck and the pot balances. If the pot is too heavy, remove some of the sprinkles so it is able to balance. Place your unicorn on the cake, if using, pressing down slightly into the icing to secure. Serve and watch the wonderment on your guest's faces!

FIREWORK CHOCOLATE CAKE

SERVES 16   PREP TIME: 1¼ HOURS, PLUS COOLING   COOK TIME: 20 MINS

This decadent chocolate sponge is the perfect celebration cake for bonfire night or New Year's Eve. Take a slice to reveal bright neon buttercream within!

75g cocoa powder

5 large eggs

1 teaspoon vanilla extract

300g self-raising flour

2 teaspoons baking powder

400g caster sugar

50ml sunflower oil

250g unsalted butter, softened, plus extra for greasing

FOR THE BUTTERCREAM

250g unsalted butter, softened

500g icing sugar, sifted

1 teaspoon vanilla extract

neon food colouring pastes (teal, purple and orange)

FOR THE CHOCOLATE GANACHE

250ml double cream

3 tablespoons golden caster sugar

400g dark chocolate (minimum 70% cocoa solids), finely chopped

TO DECORATE

75g icing sugar

neon food colouring pastes (as above, plus magenta)

1 tablespoon white nonpareils sprinkle

YOU WILL NEED

fine paintbrush

sparkler fountain or indoor sparklers

1. Preheat the oven to 180°C/gas mark 4. Grease and line 4 x 18cm round cake tins and line with baking parchment.

2. Put the cocoa in a bowl and stir in 200ml boiling water until smooth, then set aside to cool slightly. Put the eggs, vanilla extract and 90ml of cold water in a bowl and whisk together until combined. Set aside.

3. In a separate large bowl, sift the flour with the baking powder and caster sugar. Add the cocoa mixture, oil and butter. Beat together for 1 minute using an electric hand whisk, then gradually add the egg mixture, beating well after each addition. Divide the mixture between the prepared tins, spreading evenly. Bake for 20 minutes, or until a skewer inserted into the centre comes out clean. Leave to cool in the tins for 10 minutes, then turn out onto a wire rack and leave to cool completely.

4. Meanwhile, for the buttercream, beat the butter, icing sugar and vanilla extract together in a bowl until light and fluffy. Divide between three smaller bowls and colour each portion with a different food colouring paste. Once the cake layers are cold, sandwich them together with the coloured buttercreams, spreading a different coloured one between each layer.

5. For the ganache, place the cream and sugar in a non-stick saucepan. Bring just to the boil, then remove from the heat and add the chocolate. Leave for 2 minutes before gently stirring until smooth and glossy. Leave to cool and thicken slightly before spreading over the cake with a palette knife.

6. To decorate, mix the icing sugar with a few drops of cold water until you have a thick but still runny icing. Divide between four small bowls and add food colouring paste to each. Using a fine paintbrush, paint fireworks onto the cake and decorate with the white sprinkles. Leave to set in the fridge for 30 minutes before decorating with indoor sparklers.

RED VELVET RAINBOW CAKE

SERVES 10   PREP TIME: 1½ HOURS, PLUS COOLING   COOK TIME: 40 MINS

The hypnotic rows of rainbow-coloured sweets on this cake will have the kids mesmerised.

120g unsalted butter, softened, plus extra for greasing

300g caster sugar

2 large eggs

40g cocoa powder

1-2 teaspoons red food colouring paste

1 teaspoon vanilla extract

240ml buttermilk

300g plain flour

1 teaspoon bicarbonate of soda

½ teaspoon fine salt

1 tablespoon white wine vinegar

CREAM CHEESE BUTTERCREAM

200g unsalted butter, softened

250g icing sugar

200g full-fat cream cheese

½ teaspoon vanilla extract

TO DECORATE

800g mixed Original and Tropical Skittles or rainbow-coloured sweets

1. Preheat the oven to 180°C/gas mark 4. Grease a 20 x 9cm bundt tin or ring mould.

2. Using an electric hand whisk, beat the butter and caster sugar together in a medium bowl until light and fluffy. Add the eggs, one at a time, beating well after each addition. In a small bowl, combine the cocoa, food colouring paste and vanilla extract to make a thick paste. Whisk this into the butter mixture.

3. Beat in half the buttermilk until smooth and combined. Sift over the flour, bicarbonate of soda and salt and fold through evenly with a large spoon. Gently beat in the remaining buttermilk with the vinegar, then beat the whole mixture for 2 minutes.

4. Pour into the prepared bundt tin, spreading evenly. Bake for 40 minutes, or until a skewer inserted into the centre comes out clean. Leave to cool in the tin for 10 minutes, then turn out onto a wire rack and leave to cool completely.

5. For the cream cheese icing, beat the butter and icing sugar together in a bowl until light and fluffy. Gradually beat in the cream cheese, a spoonful at a time, then beat in the vanilla extract until smooth and combined.

6. Once the cake is cold, use a serrated knife to trim the base then cut it in half vertically so you have two crescents. Use some of the cream cheese icing to sandwich the flat sides of the trimmed base together and then 'stand' them up on a serving plate or board securing them with a little icing underneath so the cake is the shape of a rainbow.

7. Using a palette knife, cover the outside of the cake evenly with the remaining icing, then press the Skittles or sweets in coloured rows over the cake to look like a rainbow.

PETAL CAKE

SERVES 18   PREP TIME: 1¼ HOURS, PLUS COOLING AND CHILLING   COOK TIME: 20-25 MINUTES

Before you say 'this one's too hard I can't make it' think again. This gorgeous petal effect is much simpler to achieve than you'd imagine.

350g unsalted butter, softened,
   plus extra for greasing
350g caster sugar
6 large eggs
350g plain flour
2½ teaspoons baking powder
1 teaspoon fine salt
1 teaspoon vanilla extract
4 tablespoons whole milk

FOR THE BUTTERCREAM

750g unsalted butter, softened
1.5kg icing sugar, sifted
1 teaspoon vanilla extract
food colouring pastes (purple, blue,
   green, yellow, orange and pink)

YOU WILL NEED

ruler
cocktail stick
6 disposable piping bags

1. Preheat the oven to 180°C/gas mark 4. Grease and line 3 x 20cm round cake tins with baking parchment.

2. Using an electric hand whisk, beat the butter and caster sugar together in a large bowl until light and fluffy. Add the eggs, one at a time, beating well after each addition. Sift in the flour, baking powder and salt and fold through evenly with a large spoon. Stir in the vanilla extract and milk until combined.

3. Divide the mixture between the prepared tins, spreading evenly. Bake for 20-25 minutes, or until a skewer inserted into the centre comes out clean. Leave to cool in the tins for 5 minutes, then turn out onto a wire rack and leave to cool completely before cutting each sponge in half horizontally.

4. Meanwhile, for the buttercream, beat the butter, icing sugar and vanilla extract together in a large bowl until light and fluffy. Divide between six smaller bowls and colour each portion with a different food colouring paste. Once the cake layers are cold, sandwich them together using a few tablespoons of each different coloured buttercream between each layer, then coat the cake completely with a thin layer of yellow buttercream to catch all the crumbs.

5. Using a ruler, measure the height of your cake, then using a cocktail stick, mark the mid-height point all the way round. Chill the cake in the fridge for 1 hour.

6. Spoon each of the remaining coloured buttercreams into a separate piping bag and snip 1cm holes off the tips. Line up the bags in the order in which you want to pipe the colours, then using the marked centre guideline, pipe rows of dots onto the cake - three above the line and three below. Then, use the

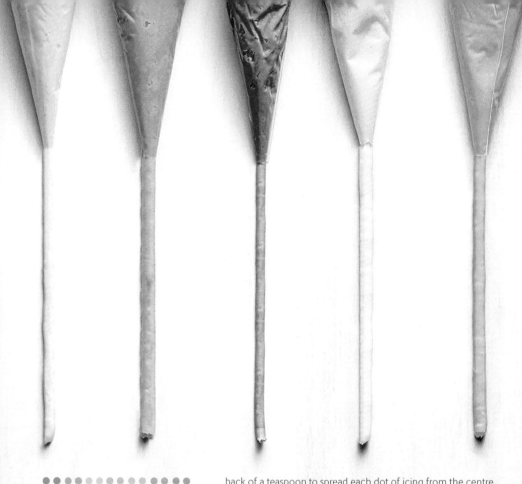

back of a teaspoon to spread each dot of icing from the centre to the right. Clean the spoon between each use.

7. Continue with your next row of dots, but move the colours all down one position, checking often to make sure your lines are vertical. Continue in this way with all the remaining coloured buttercreams but don't spread the final row of dots.

8. Pipe a circle of dots around the outer top edge of the cake. Spread these dots as before, then continue to the centre, reducing the amount of dots when it gets tight. Finish with one dot in the centre. .

POLKA DOT SURPRISE BUNDT CAKE

SERVES 14   PREP TIME: 1¼ HOURS, PLUS COOLING AND FREEZING   COOK TIME: 1½ HOURS

This cake is so impressive, but is secretly really rather easy to make.
Topped with its cheerful rainbow icing, you are bound to get plenty
of smiles from your guests.

FOR THE RAINBOW CAKE BALLS

120g unsalted butter, softened,
  plus extra for greasing
120g caster sugar
2 large eggs
120g self-raising flour
1 teaspoon lemon or orange extract
food colouring pastes (purple, blue,
  green, yellow, orange and red)

FOR THE VANILLA SPONGE

275g unsalted butter, softened
275g caster sugar
4 large eggs
275g self-raising flour
½ teaspoon fine salt
1 teaspoon vanilla extract
3 tablespoons whole milk

FOR THE BUTTERCREAM

100g white chocolate (minimum
  30% cocoa solids), roughly
  chopped
150g unsalted butter, softened
150g icing sugar, sifted
1 teaspoon vanilla extract
food colouring pastes (purple, blue,
  green, yellow, orange and pink)

1. Preheat the oven to 180°C/gas mark 4. Lightly grease the cake pop mould.

2. For the rainbow cake balls, using an electric hand whisk, beat the butter and caster sugar together in a medium bowl until light and fluffy. Add the eggs, one at a time, beating well after each addition. Sift in the flour and fold through evenly with a large spoon. Stir in the lemon or orange extract until combined.

3. Divide the mixture between six bowls and stir a little food colouring paste into each portion. Place the base of the mould on a baking tray. Carefully spoon some of the coloured batters into each hole of the prepared mould, filling each one right to the top so it rises and fills the other half of the mould during baking. Gently place the lid of the mould (with the air holes on the top) in position and secure in place.

4. Bake for 12–14 minutes. Insert a cocktail stick into a hole to check if the cakes are cooked – it should come out clean. Remove the lid and leave to cool in the mould for 10 minutes, then gently press the cakes out of the mould onto a wire rack and leave to cool completely.

5. Quickly wash and dry the mould, lightly grease again and spoon in the remaining cake mixtures (the mixture should make about 26 cake balls in total). Repeat the baking and cooling as before. Once cold, trim off any excess cake from the balls and place them on a baking tray in the freezer for 30 minutes.

YOU WILL NEED

20-hole/cup cake pop moulds
6 disposable piping bags,
  each fitted with a different
  shaped nozzle

● ● ● ● ● ● ● ● ● ● ● ● ● ● ● ●

**IF YOU DON'T HAVE A CAKE POP
MOULD, INSTEAD YOU CAN MAKE AND
BAKE THE CAKE BALL MIXTURE IN A
GREASED AND LINED 20CM ROUND
CAKE TIN (BAKE IT FOR ABOUT 15
MINUTES, THEN TURN OUT AND LEAVE
TO COOL). ONCE COLD (IDEALLY 24
HOURS LATER), BREAK THE CAKE INTO
PIECES AND DIVIDE BETWEEN SIX
SMALL BOWLS. PULSE EACH BATCH
IN A FOOD-PROCESSOR WITH
1 TABLESPOON OF THE UNCOLOURED
BUTTERCREAM AND A LITTLE FOOD
COLOURING PASTE. ROLL INTO BALLS
AND FREEZE BEFORE BAKING
IN THE CAKE.**

● ● ● ● ● ● ● ● ● ● ● ● ● ● ● ●

6. Preheat the oven again to 180°C/gas mark 4. Grease a 20 x 9cm bundt tin or ring mould. For the vanilla sponge, using an electric hand whisk, beat the butter and caster sugar together in a medium bowl until light and fluffy. Add the eggs, one at a time, beating well after each addition. Sift in the flour and salt then fold through evenly with a large spoon. Gently stir in the vanilla extract and milk until combined.

7. Spoon a small amount of cake mixture into the prepared tin, spreading evenly. Drop a few cake balls into the mixture, then cover with more cake mixture. Continue layering the cake balls and cake mixture until you have used them all up, finishing with a layer of cake mixture spread evenly.

8. Bake for 1 hour, or until a skewer inserted into the centre comes out clean. Cover the cake with foil after 30 minutes if it's browning too quickly. Leave to cool completely in the tin before turning out onto a plate.

9. For the buttercream, melt the chocolate in a heatproof bowl over a pan of barely simmering water. Leave to cool slightly. Beat the butter and icing sugar together in a separate bowl until creamy, then beat in the melted chocolate and vanilla extract until combined.

10. Divide the buttercream between six smaller bowls and stir a little food colouring paste into each portion. Spoon each coloured buttercream into a piping bag and then randomly pipe coloured swirls over the top of the cake. Slice to reveal the surprise inside and serve.

VERTICAL OMBRE CAKE

SERVES 20 PREP TIME: 2¼ HOURS, PLUS COOLING COOK TIME: 1½ HOURS

A real show stopper, which requires a little more effort, but don't be put off!
It is well worth it for the deliciously light sponge and truly fluffy buttercream.

FOR THE SWISS ROLL SPONGE CAKES

16 large eggs
400g caster sugar, plus extra
 for sprinkling
600g plain flour
3 teaspoons baking powder
160g salted butter, melted, plus
 extra for greasing
peach food colouring paste

FOR THE ROUND SPONGE CAKES

6 large eggs
150g caster sugar, plus extra
 for sprinkling
225g plain flour
1 teaspoon baking powder
60g salted butter, melted

FOR THE BUTTERCREAM

6 large egg whites
350g caster sugar
500g unsalted butter, softened,
 cut into cubes
1 teaspoon vanilla extract
peach food colouring paste

TO DECORATE

organic fresh flowers

YOU WILL NEED

sugar thermometer
large palette knife

1. Preheat the oven to 180°C/gas mark 4. Grease and line a 26 x 37cm Swiss roll tin with baking parchment.

2. For the Swiss roll sponge cakes, using an electric hand whisk, whisk 4 eggs and 100g sugar together in a medium, grease-free bowl until pale, thick and doubled in volume. Sift 150g flour and ¾ teaspoon baking powder over the egg mixture, then pour 40g melted butter down the side of the bowl. Using a large metal spoon, very gently fold in until just combined, being careful not to knock the air out.

3. Pour the mixture into your lined tin and gently smooth with a palette knife. Bake for 12–14 minutes, or until springy and dry to the touch.

4. Place a large sheet of baking parchment onto a clean surface and sprinkle with the extra caster sugar. Carefully turn out the hot sponge onto the paper, peeling away the lining paper. Loosely roll up the sponge from a short side, with the sugared paper inside, then leave to cool completely on a wire rack.

5. Repeat the steps above three more times (to make four Swiss roll sponge cakes in total), but each time adding a little peach food colouring paste to the sponge mixture, making each one slightly darker than the previous one.

6. For the round sponge cakes, grease and line 2 x 23cm round cake tins with baking parchment. Repeat step 2 above using all the ingredients listed on the left. Divide this mixture between the prepared tins, spreading evenly, then bake for 12–14 minutes, or until springy and dry to the touch. Turn out onto sugared paper and leave to cool completely on a wire rack.

7. While all the cakes cool, make the Swiss meringue buttercream. Place the egg whites and sugar into a medium, heatproof

I'VE USED A PRETTY PASTEL FOOD COLOURING PASTE BUT THIS CAKE ALSO LOOKS GREAT WITH A PUNCHIER GREEN OR BLUE OMBRE EFFECT.

bowl over a pan of simmering water. Whisk constantly until the mixture reaches 70°C on a sugar thermometer and the sugar is completely dissolved, about 10-15 minutes.

8. Transfer to a large bowl, then using an electric hand whisk, whisk for about 10 minutes, or until firm peaks form and the mixture has almost cooled to room temperature. Gradually add the butter, one cube at a time, beating well between additions, until all the butter is combined and the mixture is pale and smooth. Whisk in the vanilla extract.

9. Take one-third of the mixture and place it in a bowl. Divide the remaining buttercream evenly between three separate bowls. Add a little food colouring paste to these three bowls, making each buttercream slightly darker than the previous one.

10. Place a round sponge cake on your cake stand and spread with a thin layer of the plain buttercream. Set aside. Carefully unroll the Swiss rolls (sheet cakes) and use a knife to cut each one in half lengthways. Spread one half of the lightest sheet cake with a thin layer of plain buttercream, then roll up tightly (minus the paper this time) to create a log. Place the rolled sponge upright in the centre of the round sponge on the cake stand. You will only need one of the palest sheet cake halves, so discard the other (or use it to make a trifle or similar).

11. Take the next palest sheet cake half and spread thinly with the next shade of buttercream. Roll around the plain sponge, starting from where the first sponge ended (so joining them together). Continue with the remaining sheet cake halves, spreading them with buttercream and then rolling each one around the other, graduating from light to dark sponges. Spread a little plain buttercream over the top of the rolled sponges. Then top with your final round cake. Trim your round cakes to fit the rolled cakes.

12. Spread any remaining plain buttercream over the top of the cake, then gradually spread the lightest peach buttercream over the top third of the cake, spread the next shade over the middle third of the cake, then finally, spread the darkest shade over the lower third of the cake. Use a long palette knife to gently blend the colours together. Decorate with fresh flowers and serve.

RAINBOW YULE LOG

SERVES 8   PREP TIME: 45 MINUTES, PLUS COOLING   COOK TIME: 12-14 MINUTES

Break from tradition and serve the brightest, most beautiful
Christmas Yule log anyone has ever seen!

4 large eggs

100g caster sugar, plus extra
for sprinkling

food colouring pastes (purple, blue,
green, yellow, orange and red)

150g plain flour

¾ teaspoon baking powder

40g unsalted butter, melted
and cooled

FOR THE WHIPPED CREAM FILLING

250ml whipping cream

50g icing sugar, plus extra
for dusting

½ teaspoon vanilla extract

YOU WILL NEED

6 disposable piping bags
a clean tea towel

1. Preheat the oven to 180°C/gas mark 4. Grease and line a 26 x
   37cm Swiss roll tin with baking parchment.

2. Using an electric hand whisk, whisk the eggs and caster sugar
   together in a medium bowl until pale, thick and doubled in
   volume. Working quickly, gently divide the mixture between six
   smaller bowls and stir a food colouring paste into each portion.

3. Sift the flour and baking powder into a separate bowl to
   combine evenly. Sprinkle 3 tablespoons of the flour mixture
   over each portion of coloured egg mixture with a drizzle of
   the melted butter, then fold it in very gently with a metal spoon
   until just combined, being careful not to knock the air out.

4. Gently spoon each coloured mixture into a separate piping
   bag, then cut off each tip to create a 2cm hole. Pipe lines
   of the mixtures diagonally across the prepared tin in a
   rainbow pattern, making sure the lines touch each other, and
   continuing until the tin is full and all the mixture is used up.
   Bake for 12-14 minutes, or until springy and dry to the touch.

5. Place a large sheet of baking parchment onto a clean
   surface and sprinkle with caster sugar. Carefully turn out the
   hot sponge onto the paper, peeling away the lining paper.
   Loosely roll up the sponge from a short side, with the sugared
   paper inside, wrap with a damp tea towel, then leave to cool
   completely on a wire rack.

6. For the whipped cream filling, pour the cream into a large
   bowl and, using an electric hand whisk, whip the cream until
   soft peaks form. Sift over the icing sugar and add the vanilla
   extract, then whisk again briefly until just combined.

7. Gently unroll the sponge cake and spread evenly with the
   cream filling. Re-roll the sponge (minus the paper), finishing
   with the join underneath. Dust with icing sugar before serving.

SMALL BAKES

OVER THE RAINBOW CUPCAKES

MAKES 12   PREP TIME: 40 MINUTES, PLUS COOLING   COOK TIME: 20 MINUTES

Find your pot of gold at the end of the rainbow with these delightful
multi-coloured rainbow layered cupcakes.

175g unsalted butter, softened
175g caster sugar
3 large eggs
175g self-raising flour
½ teaspoon fine salt
1 teaspoon vanilla extract
2 tablespoons whole milk
food colouring pastes (purple, blue,
    green, yellow, orange and red)

FOR THE ICING

150g unsalted butter, softened
300g icing sugar, sifted
200g white marshmallow fluff

TO DECORATE

6 rainbow fizzy belts, halved
edible gold dust

YOU WILL NEED

12 cupcake cases
disposable piping bag fitted with
    a 1cm round nozzle

1. Preheat the oven to 180°C/gas mark 4. Line a 12-hole muffin tin
    with cupcake cases.

2. Using an electric hand whisk, beat the butter and caster sugar
    together in a medium bowl until light and fluffy. Add the eggs,
    one at a time, beating well after each addition. Sift in the flour
    and salt and fold through evenly with a large spoon. Stir in the
    vanilla extract and milk until combined.

3. Divide the mixture between six bowls. Stir a little food
    colouring paste into each portion. Divide the purple cake
    mixture between the cupcake cases and spread evenly. Top this
    with the blue cake mixture, spreading evenly on top. Continue
    in this way with the remaining cake mixtures (green, yellow,
    orange, then red), so that you end up with rainbow layers in
    each cupcake case.

4. Bake for 20 minutes, or until the cakes are risen and spring back
    when lightly pressed. Leave to cool in the tins for 5 minutes,
    then transfer to a wire rack and leave to cool completely.

5. Meanwhile, for the icing, beat the butter and icing sugar
    together in a bowl until light and fluffy. Add the marshmallow
    fluff and beat until smooth and combined.

6. Once the cupcakes are cold, spoon the icing into the piping
    bag and pipe swirls of icing onto each cupcake. Decorate
    with the rainbow belts and gold dust just before serving.

RAINBOW TOWERS

MAKES 15　PREP TIME: 1 HOUR, PLUS COOLING AND CHILLING　COOK TIME: 30-45 MINUTES

Layers of rainbow sponge are sandwiched together, then cut into squares.
Perfect for an afternoon treat and a nice change from the classic cupcake.

750g unsalted butter, softened, plus
　extra for greasing
750g caster sugar
9 large eggs, lightly beaten
750g self-raising flour
1 teaspoon fine salt
100ml whole milk
2 teaspoons vanilla extract
food colouring pastes (purple, blue,
　green, yellow, orange and red)

FOR THE CREAM CHEESE ICING

300g unsalted butter, softened
375g icing sugar, sifted
300g full-fat cream cheese
1 teaspoon vanilla extract

1. Preheat the oven to 180°C/gas mark 4. Grease and line two 26 x 37cm Swiss roll tins with baking parchment.

2. Using an electric hand whisk, beat the butter and caster sugar together in a large bowl until light and fluffy. Gradually add the eggs, beating well after each addition. Sift in the flour and salt and fold through evenly with a large spoon. Stir in the milk and vanilla extract until combined.

3. Weigh the mixture, then divide it evenly between six smaller bowls. Add a different food colouring paste to each bowl, adding a little at a time and stirring until you reach your required colours. Spoon two of the coloured cake mixtures into the prepared tins, spreading evenly.

4. Bake for 10-15 minutes, or until a skewer inserted into the centre comes out clean. Leave to cool in the tins for 5 minutes, then turn out onto wire racks and leave to cool completely. Quickly wash and dry, then re-grease and line the tins. Spoon two more of the coloured cake mixtures into the tins and spread evenly, then bake and cool as before. Repeat this step one final time to bake the final two cakes.

5. While the cakes are cooling, make the cream cheese icing. Beat the butter and icing sugar together in a bowl until light and fluffy. Gradually beat in the cream cheese, a spoonful at a time, then beat in the vanilla extract until smooth and combined.

6. Once all the cakes are cold, sandwich the cake layers together, spreading a layer of icing between each one, starting with the purple sponge, then the blue, green, yellow, orange and red ones. Chill in the fridge for 1 hour.

7. Use a serrated knife to trim the edges and then cut the cake into 15 squares to serve.

RAINBOW CAKE IN A JAR

SERVES 1   PREP TIME: 20 MINUTES, PLUS COOLING   COOK TIME: 20–25 MINUTES

This one is for when it's just you and you can't trust yourself with a whole cake in the house! Baked individually in a jar, it's soon ready to enjoy and there's no need to share it.

75g unsalted butter, softened, plus extra for greasing
75g caster sugar
1 large egg
75g self-raising flour
pinch of fine salt
¼ teaspoon vanilla extract
food colouring pastes (purple, blue, green, yellow, orange and red)

FOR THE ICING
50ml double cream
1 teaspoon icing sugar, sifted
¼ teaspoon vanilla extract
1 teaspoon edible confetti or rainbow sprinkles

YOU WILL NEED
1 x 400ml ovenproof glass jar

1. Preheat the oven to 180°C/gas mark 4.

2. Using an electric hand whisk, beat the butter and caster sugar together in a medium bowl until light and fluffy. Add the egg, beating well, then sift in the flour and salt and fold through evenly with a spoon. Stir in the vanilla extract until combined.

3. Divide the mixture between six small bowls. Stir a little food colouring paste into each portion. Spoon the coloured cake mixtures into the prepared jar, spooning them one on top of the other and working your way through the rainbow – purple, blue, green, yellow, orange and red.

4. Bake for 20–25 minutes, or until a skewer inserted into the centre comes out clean. Set the jar aside to cool completely.

5. For the icing, whip the cream, icing sugar and vanilla extract together in a small bowl until soft peaks form. Once the cake is cold, spoon the icing over the cake and scatter with edible confetti or rainbow sprinkles before serving.

PASTEL CUPCAKES

MAKES 12   PREP TIME: 25 MINUTES, PLUS COOLING   COOK TIME: 20 MINUTES

Bite into these playful cupcakes, topped with a dreamy pastel icing,
to reveal the swirl of rainbow colours inside.

225g unsalted butter, softened
225g caster sugar
zest of 1 orange
zest of 1 lemon
3 large eggs
225g plain flour
1½ teaspoons baking powder
½ teaspoon fine salt
1 teaspoon orange extract
food colouring pastes (blue, green,
    yellow and pink)

FOR THE BUTTERCREAM

250g unsalted butter, softened
500g icing sugar, sifted
food colouring pastes (as above)

YOU WILL NEED

12 cupcake cases
large piping bag fitted with an
    open star nozzle

1. Preheat the oven to 180°C/gas mark 4. Line a 12-hole muffin tin with cupcake cases.

2. Using an electric hand whisk, beat the butter and caster sugar together in a medium bowl until light and fluffy. Beat in the citrus zests, then add the eggs, one at a time, beating well after each addition. Sift in the flour, baking powder and salt and fold through evenly with a large spoon. Stir in the orange extract until combined.

3. Divide the mixture between four bowls. Stir a little food colouring paste into each portion. Place spoonfuls of the coloured mixtures randomly into the cupcake cases, then gently drag a skewer through the mixture two or three times to give a marbled effect.

4. Bake for 20 minutes until the cakes are risen and spring back when lightly pressed. Leave to cool in the tins for 5 minutes, then transfer to a wire rack and leave to cool completely.

5. For the buttercream, beat the butter and icing sugar together in a medium bowl until light and fluffy. Divide between four smaller bowls and colour each portion with a different food colouring paste.

6. Take the piping bag and roll it down halfway. Add a spoonful of one of the four coloured buttercreams to the bottom of the bag, making sure you leave space for the three others by its side – as you want all the colours to pipe out at the same time. Add a spoonful of the second coloured buttercream, alongside the first, trying to push the icing down to the same point in the bag as the first. Repeat with the third and fourth colours, filling the bottom of the bag. Continue adding the buttercream colours in the same places (placing each layer of four buttercreams on

top of the previous one), avoiding creating air pockets, until the bag is three-quarters full and all the buttercream is used up. Roll up the rest of the bag and twist the top to secure.

7. Once the cupcakes are cold, pipe some buttercream on top of each cupcake in a spiral pattern, working from the outside edge inwards and keeping constant pressure on the icing bag. Continue the spiral pattern, into a second layer of icing on top of the first working gradually towards the centre. To finish, release the pressure on the bag, press down lightly then pull straight up to get a nice finish.

SPRINKLE WITH EDIBLE GLITTER FOR AN EVEN MORE MAGICAL FEEL.

EASTER EGG CAKE POPS

MAKES 30 PREP TIME: 1¼ HOURS, PLUS COOLING, FREEZING, CHILLING AND SETTING COOK TIME: 20 MINUTES

Take a break from all the chocolate at Easter and enjoy some delicious vanilla-speckled egg cake pops instead!

250g unsalted butter, softened, plus
   extra for greasing
250g caster sugar
4 large eggs
250g self-raising flour
½ teaspoon fine salt
1 teaspoon vanilla extract
2 tablespoons whole milk

FOR THE BUTTERCREAM

150g unsalted butter
300g icing sugar, sifted

TO DECORATE

1kg coloured candy melts (200g
   of each colour in blue, green,
   yellow, orange and pink)
2 vanilla pods, split in half
   lengthways and seeds scraped out
2½ teaspoons vegetable oil
   (optional)

YOU WILL NEED

30 long lollipop sticks
cake pop stand (or a Styrofoam
   block to stand the cake pops up
   in when they are decorated)

1. Preheat the oven to 180°C/gas mark 4. Grease and line 2 x 20cm round cake tins with baking parchment.

2. Using an electric hand whisk, beat the butter and caster sugar together in a large bowl until light and fluffy. Add the eggs, one at a time, beating well after each addition. Sift in the flour and salt and fold through evenly with a large spoon. Stir in the vanilla extract and milk until combined.

3. Divide the mixture between the prepared tins, spreading evenly. Bake for 20 minutes, or until a skewer inserted into the centre comes out clean. Leave to cool in the tins for 5 minutes, then turn out onto a wire rack and leave to cool completely.

4. Meanwhile, to make the buttercream, whisk the butter and icing sugar together with an electric mixer until light and fluffy.

5. Once the cakes are cold, finely crumble them into a large bowl and then stir through the buttercream, mixing until well combined. Taking small portions – about a heaped tablespoonful of the mixture – roll each portion into an egg shape, making 30 eggs in total. Place on a tray and freeze for about 15 minutes until firm but not frozen, then transfer all the cake pops to the fridge so they stay chilled.

6. Place one batch (one colour) of the coloured candy melts in a medium heatproof bowl over a small saucepan of barely simmering water. Make sure the water doesn't touch the base of the bowl and be careful not to overheat the candy melts as they can burn easily. Add one-fifth of the vanilla seeds and then stir occasionally until the mixture is melted and smooth – if it is a little thick, add ½ teaspoon of vegetable oil to make it more fluid.

7. Take six cake pops out of the fridge. Dip a lollipop stick into the melted icing, then push it about 2cm into a cake pop. Dip the entire cake pop into the icing, turning to coat it all over. Try to do this in one motion, because if you keep re-dipping the cake pop, it may come off the stick. Gently rotate the lollipop stick to allow excess icing to drip off, then stick the cake pop into the stand or Styrofoam block. Repeat with the remaining five cake pops and melted icing.

8. Repeat steps 5 and 6 above for each batch of coloured candy melts and each batch of six cake pops, melting each icing separately and coating the cake pops with the icing. Leave the cake pops to set completely before serving.

GLAZED RING DOUGHNUTS

MAKES 16   PREP TIME: 50 MINUTES, PLUS RISING, PROVING AND COOLING   COOK TIME: 20-25 MINUTES

These doughnuts are light and chewy and guaranteed to get even the laziest person out of bed at the weekend!

500g strong white bread flour, plus extra for dusting

50g caster sugar

1 teaspoon fine salt

100g unsalted butter, chilled and cubed

7g sachet fast-action dried yeast

160ml warm (hand-hot) water

2 large eggs, lightly beaten

2 litres sunflower oil for deep-frying, plus extra for greasing

TO DECORATE

400g icing sugar

food colouring pastes (blue, green, yellow, orange pink and red)

YOU WILL NEED

3cm round pastry cutter

kitchen thermometer

DEEP-FRY THE CENTRE CUT-OUTS FROM THE DOUGHNUTS IN THE HOT OIL FOR 1-2 MINUTES, THEN DRAIN AND SERVE WARM OR COLD, TOSSED IN EXTRA CASTER SUGAR, IF YOU LIKE.

1. Lightly grease a large bowl and grease two baking trays. Sift the flour, sugar and salt into a large bowl and then using your fingertips, rub in the butter until the mixture resembles breadcrumbs. Fold through the dried yeast.

2. Pour over the warm water and mix until combined. Then add the eggs and mix with a wooden spoon until the mixture forms a dough. Turn out onto a lightly floured surface and knead for 10 minutes by hand (or alternatively, use a stand mixer fitted with a dough hook) until the dough springs back when pressed.

3. Place the dough in the greased bowl and cover loosely with oiled clingfilm. Leave to rise in a warm place for 1-2 hours, or until doubled in size.

4. Knock the air out of the risen dough by kneading it for 2 minutes on a floured surface. Divide the dough into 16 equal pieces, then shape each one into a smooth ball (do this by rolling each one on the surface with the palm of your hand). Place the dough balls on the prepared baking trays, leaving room for them to expand as they prove. Cover loosely with oiled clingfilm and leave to prove in a warm place for a further 1 hour, or until doubled in size.

5. Lightly oil the pastry cutter and use it to stamp out the middle of each doughnut. Discard the centres or see Cook's Tips, left, for how to make mini doughnuts from the centres!

6. Pour the sunflower oil into a large, deep saucepan and heat the oil to 160°C, using the thermometer to check it's hot enough. Drop two or three doughnuts into the oil, one at a time, and deep-fry on each side for 2-3 minutes, or until golden-brown. Remove with a slotted spoon and place on a plate lined with kitchen paper to soak up the excess oil. Repeat with the

remaining doughnuts (ensuring the oil is brought back up to temperature for each batch) until they are all cooked.

7. To make the icing, put the icing sugar in a bowl and stir in 4–5 tablespoons of cold water until smooth – you want a thick but still runny consistency. Divide the mixture into six smaller bowls, then stir a little food colouring paste into each portion.

8. Using a teaspoon, draw a 1cm thick line of one of the coloured icings, onto a plate, just longer than the width of your doughnuts, then repeat with the remaining coloured icings, placing them side by side (with all the lines touching to create a square-ish rainbow). Press the base of one of the cooled doughnuts into the icing and gently drag and lift to the side. Dragging is important to get the icing to stick to the doughnut. Dip another doughnut into the icings in the same way. Set them aside on a serving plate.

9. Repeat with the remaining coloured icings and doughnuts, remembering to refresh your icing lines on the plate after every two doughnuts.

10. Leave the decorated doughnuts to set for 30 minutes–1 hour somewhere cool (but not the fridge). These doughnuts are best eaten fresh, though you can store them in an airtight container (with greaseproof paper between each layer) for up to 3 days.

FRECKLE CINNAMON ROLLS

MAKES 16   PREP TIME: 40 MINUTES, PLUS RISING AND PROVING   COOK TIME: 15-20 MINUTES

Rainbow strands or jimmies really liven up this classic recipe and these tasty sweet rolls are a real treat for the weekend.

300ml whole milk

6 cardamom pods, husks removed and seeds ground

50g butter

450g strong white bread flour, plus extra for dusting

7g sachet fast-action dried yeast

50g caster sugar

½ teaspoon fine salt

2 large eggs

flavourless oil (such as sunflower), for greasing

FOR THE CINNAMON FILLING

100g salted butter, softened

80g soft light brown sugar

1 tablespoon ground cinnamon

zest of 1 orange

65g rainbow jimmies (a large thicker version of vermicelli) – I use Wilton's

FOR THE DRIZZLE ICING AND DECORATION

50g icing sugar, sifted

15g rainbow jimmies

1. Heat the milk in a small saucepan with the ground cardamom seeds. Bring just to the boil, then remove from the heat and stir in the butter until melted. Set aside until the mixture has cooled to lukewarm.

2. Meanwhile, sift the flour, yeast, caster sugar and salt into a large bowl. Make a well in the centre and mix in 1 egg (reserve the remaining egg for the glaze). Pour the flavoured milk into the bowl and stir until it comes together to form a soft, sticky dough.

3. Lightly oil a clean surface with 1–2 teaspoons of oil. Turn the dough onto the oiled surface (or alternatively, use a stand mixer fitted with a dough hook) and knead for 10 minutes until it's smooth and springs back a little. The dough will be very sticky to begin with but don't add any extra flour as it will get less sticky as you knead. Transfer the dough to a clean, lightly greased bowl. Cover with a clean tea-towel and leave to rise in a warm place for 30 minutes, until nearly doubled in size.

4. For the cinnamon filling, beat the butter, sugar, cinnamon and orange zest together in a bowl until soft and spreadable. Lightly flour a clean surface and dust your hands with flour. Tip out the dough and turn once to lightly coat in the flour, then roll it out into a 35 x 25cm rectangle, with one of the longer sides closest to you.

5. Using your fingers and a palette knife, spread the cinnamon mixture over the dough right up to the edges, then scatter over the jimmies. Roll up the dough fairly tightly, starting with the long edge closest to you. Finish with the seam underneath, then cut into 16 even slices.

6. Grease a deep, round cake tin, about 30cm in diameter or a 35 x 25cm roasting tin. Place the cinnamon buns into the prepared tin, spacing them evenly. Cover with the tea-towel and leave to prove in a warm place for a further 30 minutes until the buns have puffed up and are now touching each other. Meanwhile, preheat the oven to 180°C/gas mark 4.

7. Beat the remaining egg and lightly brush it over the cinnamon buns. Bake for 15–20 minutes until golden-brown. Leave in the tin for 10 minutes, then turn out onto a wire rack and leave to cool completely.

8. To make the drizzle icing, in a small bowl, mix the icing sugar with 1–2 teaspoons of cold water, stirring to make a thick but drizzling consistency. Drizzle over the cold buns, then scatter generously with the rainbow jimmies before serving.

MULTI-COLOURED BAGELS

MAKES 12   PREP TIME: 1 HOUR, PLUS RISING, PROVING AND COOLING   COOK TIME: 25 MINUTES

Brighten your breakfast table by serving up some of these dreamy bagels that are just bursting with colour. Lightly toasted, then spread with funfetti cream cheese, you are in for a real treat!

750g strong white bread flour, plus more for dusting

2 x 7g packet active dry yeast

2 teaspoons fine salt

3 tablespoons granulated sugar

500ml warm (hand-hot) water

food colouring pastes (orange, pink, purple and green)

1 teaspoon vegetable oil

FOR FUNFETTI CREAM CHEESE

280g cream cheese

75g icing sugar

2 tablespoons rainbow sprinkles

PACKED IN AN AIRTIGHT CONTAINER (WITH GREASEPROOF PAPER BETWEEN EACH LAYER), THESE BAGELS WILL KEEP WELL IN A COOL, DRY PLACE FOR UP TO 4 DAYS. ALTERNATIVELY, THEY FREEZE WELL FOR UP TO 3 MONTHS (DEFROST BEFORE SERVING). IF STORING THE BAGELS, SIMPLY MAKE THE FUNFETTI CREAM CHEESE JUST BEFORE SERVING.

1. Pour the flour, yeast, salt and sugar into a large bowl and mix to combine. Pour over the warm water and stir with a wooden spoon until the mixture forms a stiff dough. Turn the dough onto a lightly floured surface (or alternatively, use a stand mixer fitted with a dough hook) and knead for about 10 minutes until the dough is no longer sticky, adding a little extra flour if needed.

2. Divide and shape the dough into four even balls and then knead a little food colouring paste into each portion.

3. Use 1 teaspoon of oil to grease four medium bowls, then place a portion of coloured dough in each of them, turning to lightly coat in oil. Cover each bowl with lightly greased clingfilm and leave to rise in a warm place for 30 minutes.

4. Lightly grease two or three baking trays and set aside. Knock back the dough by hitting it with your fist (to knock the air out), then re-roll into balls as before. On a sheet of baking parchment, roll out each ball into a 2cm-thick rectangle, about 15 x 30cm in size. Stack the four coloured doughs on top of each other on one of the prepared baking trays, then lightly cover with greased clingfilm and leave to prove in a warm place for a further 30 minutes.

5. Slice the proved stacked doughs into 12 strips, each about 2.5 x 15cm. Twist each strip of dough a little to create a spiral and join the ends together. Repeat with the remaining dough and place on the prepared baking trays. Cover loosely with the greased cling film, then leave to prove again for another 30 minutes, or until proved back into their pre-twist size.

6. Preheat the oven to 200°C/gas mark 6. Bring a large saucepan of water to the boil. Working in batches of two or three at a time, cook the bagels in the boiling water for 30 seconds each side, turning once. Remove with a slotted spoon, drain on kitchen paper, then transfer back to the greased baking trays.

7. Once all the bagels are ready, transfer them to the oven and bake for 16 minutes, turning them over halfway through baking. The bagels should colour slightly but not brown. Transfer to a wire rack and leave to cool completely.

8. For the funfetti cream cheese, beat the cream cheese and icing sugar together in a bowl until smooth. Gently fold in the rainbow sprinkles.

9. Once the bagels are cold, cut each one in half horizontally, then lightly toast and serve spread with the funfetti cream cheese.

BISCUITS & COOKIES

COOKIE KISSES

MAKES 50 PREP TIME: 45 MINUTES, PLUS CHILLING, COOLING AND SETTING COOK TIME: 8 MINUTES

Bag up these colourful iced jewels to give to friends and brighten their day with a little rainbow happiness.

75g unsalted butter
30g caster sugar
½ teaspoon vanilla extract
115g plain flour, plus extra
　for dusting
pinch of fine salt

FOR THE ICING

250g royal icing sugar
food colouring pastes (purple, blue,
　green, yellow, orange and pink)

YOU WILL NEED

2cm cookie cutter
6 disposable piping bags
1cm open star nozzle

PACKED INTO AN AIRTIGHT
CONTAINER AND STORED IN A
COOL, DRY PLACE, THESE WILL
KEEP WELL FOR UP TO A MONTH.
STACK THEM CAREFULLY, WITH
GREASEPROOF PAPER BETWEEN
EACH LAYER.

1. Line two or three baking trays with baking parchment. Set side. Using an electric hand whisk, beat the butter, caster sugar and vanilla extract together in a medium bowl until just combined. Sift over the flour and salt and stir gently until the mixture comes together to form a dough.

2. Turn out onto a lightly floured surface and roll out to 5mm thickness. Cut out 50 rounds using the cookie cutter (or I use the base of a large piping nozzle), re-rolling the scraps. Transfer to the baking trays, then chill in the fridge for 20 minutes.

3. Preheat the oven to 180°C/gas mark 4. Remove the cookies from the fridge and bake for 8 minutes until very lightly golden. Leave to cool completely on the baking trays.

4. For the icing, sift the icing sugar into a medium bowl, then add 1 tablespoon of cold water. Using an electric hand whisk, gently whisk them together for 2–3 minutes until you have a smooth, thick icing (like the consistency of toothpaste!) – add an extra drop or two of water if the icing is too stiff.

5. Divide the icing into six small bowls and stir a little food colouring paste into each one. Fill up one piping bag, fitted with the star nozzle, with one colour of icings, then pipe stars onto some of the cookies. Clean the nozzle, insert into a clean piping bag, then repeat with another coloured icing. Repeat this process with the remaining coloured icings, so that you end up with cookies decorated with different coloured stars. Leave to set in a cool place for at least 2 hours before serving.

FUNFETTI COOKIES WITH MARSHMALLOW BUTTERCREAM

MAKES 20 PREP TIME: 40 MINUTES, PLUS CHILLING AND COOLING COOK TIME: 12-14 MINUTES

These simple shortbread biscuits, sandwiched together with scrumptious marshmallow buttercream are sure to get the party started!

225g unsalted butter, softened, plus extra for greasing
110g caster sugar
225g plain flour, plus extra for dusting
100g cornflour
½ teaspoon fine salt
75g rainbow Jimmies

FOR THE MARSHMALLOW BUTTERCREAM

150g unsalted butter
300g icing sugar
200g marshmallow fluff
food colouring pastes (purple, blue, green, yellow, orange, pink)

YOU WILL NEED

5cm round fluted cutter
piping bag fitted with 1cm round nozzle

● ● ● ● ● ● ● ● ● ● ● ● ● ● ●

THESE FREEZE WELL UNFILLED. STACK AS IN STEP 6 IN AN AIRTIGHT CONTAINER AND FREEZE FOR UP TO 3 MONTHS. DEFROST AT ROOM TEMPERATURE BEFORE SANDWICHING TOGETHER WITH BUTTERCREAM.

● ● ● ● ● ● ● ● ● ● ● ● ● ● ●

1. Using an electric hand whisk, beat the butter and sugar together in a medium bowl until light and fluffy. Sift over the flour, cornflour and salt and beat again until smooth and combined. Fold through the rainbow jimmies, then turn out onto a lightly floured surface and gently knead until you have a soft dough.

2. Using two large sheets of baking parchment, roll out the dough between the sheets to 5mm thickness. Transfer the dough (still between the sheets of paper) to a tray and chill in the fridge for 1 hour to firm up.

3. Preheat the oven to 180°C/gas mark 4. Line three large baking trays with baking parchment. Remove the cookie dough from the fridge and discard the top sheet of paper. Using the cookie cutter, cut out 40 biscuits (re-rolling the scraps) and place them on the prepared trays.

4. Bake for 12-14 minutes until golden brown at the edges. Leave to cool on the baking trays for 10 minutes until firm, then transfer to a wire rack and leave to cool completely.

5. Meanwhile, for the buttercream, beat the butter and icing sugar together in a bowl until light and fluffy. Add the marshmallow fluff and beat until smooth and combined. Divide the mixture between six smaller bowls and add food colouring to each.

6. Spoon the coloured buttercreams randomly into the piping bag. Pipe swirls of marshmallow buttercream onto the base of half the biscuits, then sandwich these together with the remaining biscuits. Packed in airtight containers they will keep well in a cool, dry place for up to 1 week. Stack them carefully, with greaseproof paper between each layer.

RAINBOW COOKIES ON STICKS

MAKES 40   PREP TIME: 1 HOUR, PLUS CHILLING, COOLING AND SETTING   COOK TIME: 10 MINUTES

The novelty of eating something off a lollipop stick is something all children seem to adore.

200g unsalted soft butter, softened

200g caster sugar

zest of 1 orange

1 large egg, lightly beaten

400g plain flour, plus extra
for dusting

FOR THE ICING

350g royal icing sugar

food colour pastes (purple, blue,
green, orange, yellow and red)

YOU WILL NEED

7 x 5cm rainbow cookie cutter

40 paper or wooden lollipop sticks

7 disposable piping bags

2mm round nozzle

PACKED INTO AN AIRTIGHT
CONTAINER AND STORED IN A COOL,
DRY PLACE, THESE COOKIES WILL
KEEP WELL FOR UP TO 2 WEEKS.
STACK THEM CAREFULLY, WITH
GREASEPROOF PAPER BETWEEN
EACH LAYER.

1. Using an electric hand whisk, beat the butter, caster sugar and orange zest together in a medium bowl until just combined and becoming creamy (don't overwork, otherwise the cookies will spread during baking). Add the egg and beat until combined. Sift in the flour and stir gently until the mixture comes together to form a dough. Shape into a ball, then cut in half and wrap each portion in clingfilm. Chill in the fridge for 1 hour.

2. Line three large baking trays with baking parchment, then set aside. On a lightly floured surface, roll out the dough to 5mm thickness. Using the cookie cutter, cut out 40 cookies, then transfer them to the prepared baking trays. Insert a lollipop stick into centre of each cookie, making sure it is covered in cookie dough. Chill in the fridge again for 30 minutes, or speed things up by chilling them in the freezer for 15 minutes.

3. Meanwhile, preheat the oven to 180°C/gas mark 4. Remove the cookies from the fridge and bake for 10 minutes until golden-brown at the edges. Cool slightly on the baking trays, then transfer the cookies to a wire rack and leave to cool completely.

4. For the icing, sift the icing sugar into a large bowl. Add 2 teaspoons of cold water and, using an electric hand whisk, whisk on a low speed for 3 minutes until you have a smooth icing that holds soft peaks (use a low speed as you don't want to incorporate too much air into the icing). Cover the bowl with a damp cloth or clingfilm to prevent the icing from drying out.

5. Once the cookies are cold, spoon 5 tablespoons of the icing into a piping bag fitted with the nozzle and pipe the outlines of the white clouds onto each cookie. Squeeze any remaining icing from the piping bag into a bowl and add extra icing so you have about 5 tablespoons of icing. Add a few drops of cold water to make the icing thick but runny enough to smooth into the edges of the clouds. Spoon back into the used piping bag

and fill in the clouds, smoothing the icing to the edges. Leave to set hard somewhere cool (but not the fridge).

6. Divide the remaining icing into six bowls and stir a little food colouring paste into each portion to make the colours of the rainbow. Make sure the icing is thick enough to pipe and only spread a little. Spoon each coloured icing into a piping bag, then cut off a 5mm tip from each one. First pipe a line of red icing across the top of each cookie between the clouds. Then, making sure you leave space for the orange line, pipe the yellow line. Leaving space for the green line, pipe the blue line, but remember to also leave space at the base for the purple line. By the time you have piped all these three lines onto all the cookies, the first batch of cookies iced will be slightly set, so you can continue and fill in the orange, green and purple lines. Leave to set hard somewhere cool for at least 4 hours. Serve the cookies on sticks in sweetie jars or in a cake pop stand.

DISCO DIP VALENTINE COOKIES

MAKES 30   PREP TIME: 1 HOUR, PLUS CHILLING AND COOLING   COOK TIME: 10 MINUTES

These cute heart-shaped cookies make a great gift for loved ones.

200g unsalted butter, softened
200g caster sugar
1 vanilla pod, split in half
    and seeds scraped out
1 large egg, lightly beaten
400g plain flour, plus extra
    for dusting

FOR THE ICING

500g royal icing sugar
food colouring pastes (blue,
    green, yellow, orange and pink)

TO DECORATE

3 tablespoons rainbow sprinkles

YOU WILL NEED

7cm heart cookie cutter
6 disposable piping bags
2mm fine round nozzle

IF YOU WANT TO COOK HALF A BATCH, FREEZE 1 BALL OF DOUGH, ONCE WRAPPED WITH CLINGFILM, OR PACK UNCOOKED OR COOKED BISCUITS INTO CONTAINERS AND FREEZE FOR UP TO 3 MONTHS. MAKE SURE TO HALVE THE ICING QUANTITY AS WELL.

1. Using an electric hand whisk, beat the butter, caster sugar and vanilla seeds together in a bowl until just combined and becoming creamy (don't overwork, otherwise the cookies will spread during baking). Add the egg and beat until combined. Sift in the flour and stir gently until the mixture comes together to form a dough. Shape into a ball, then cut in half and wrap each portion in clingfilm. Chill in the fridge for 1 hour.

2. Line two or three large baking trays with baking parchment, then set aside. On a lightly floured surface, roll out the dough to 5mm thickness. Using the cookie cutter, cut out 30 cookies, then transfer them to the baking trays. Chill in the fridge for 30 minutes, or chill them in the freezer for 15 minutes.

3. Meanwhile, preheat the oven to 180°C/gas mark 4. Remove the cookies from the fridge and bake for 10 minutes until golden-brown at the edges. Cool slightly on the baking trays, then transfer the cookies to a wire rack and leave to cool completely.

4. For the icing, sift the icing sugar into a large bowl. Add 2 teaspoons of cold water and, using an electric hand whisk, whisk on a low speed for 3 minutes until you have a smooth icing that holds soft peaks. Cover the bowl with a damp cloth or clingfilm to prevent the icing from drying out.

5. Once the cookies are cold, spoon 5 tablespoons of the icing into a piping bag fitted with the nozzle, you can just snip a small 2mm tip off the end but a nozzle gives you more control. Pipe the white sections by tracing the inner edge of the base of the heart and drawing a wiggly line across the centre.

6. Spoon ⅓ of the icing into a bowl and add ½ teaspoon of water at a time to make flood icing – a thick, runny icing that smoothes out on its own within 15 seconds. Fill the outlines with the runny icing. Divide the remaining icing into five bowls and stir a little food colouring paste into each of them. Spoon some

of each icing into separate piping bags fitted with a 2mm nozzle or just snip off the tip to make a small 2mm hole. Using the different icings, pipe a line around the inner edge of the top of the hearts joining them to the edges of the white piping. You will get six of each coloured cookie.

7. Once all the biscuits have been outlined add a little water to each of the coloured icings and fill in the hearts. Carefully scatter the tops with rainbow sprinkles and leave to set hard somewhere cool (but not the fridge) for at least 4 hours.

STAINED WINDOW GINGERBREAD BISCUITS

MAKES 35   PREP TIME: 40 MINUTES, PLUS COOLING, CHILLING AND FREEZING   COOK TIME: 6-10 MINUTES

Tie these spicy biscuits with pretty coloured ribbon or raffia and hang them on trees or in windows, so the sun can light up their rainbow centres.

70g golden syrup or clear honey

100g soft light brown sugar

100g unsalted butter

zest of ½ lemon

2 teaspoons ground ginger

1 teaspoon ground cinnamon

¼ teaspoon ground nutmeg

⅛ teaspoon ground cloves

½ teaspoon bicarbonate of soda

300g plain flour, sifted, plus extra
   for dusting

1 medium egg, lightly beaten

150–200g fruit-flavoured boiled
   sweets in different colours, each
   colour crushed separately

YOU WILL NEED

Christmas-themed cutter(s) of
   your choice

smaller round or other shaped
   cutters

drinking straw

rainbow-coloured ribbon or raffia

1. Place the syrup or honey, sugar, butter, lemon zest and ground spices in a large, heavy-based saucepan and melt over a low-medium heat, stirring frequently until the sugar has dissolved. Increase the heat and bring the mixture to the boil, then remove from the heat and beat in the bicarbonate of soda. The mixture will froth up at this point as the bicarbonate reacts, so stir it briefly, then set aside to cool for 15 minutes.

2. Fold the flour into the melted mixture in batches, using a wooden spoon or a stand mixer. Finally, beat in the egg until combined. The dough will be sticky, but scrape it out of the bowl onto a very lightly floured surface and knead until smooth. Wrap in clingfilm and chill in the fridge for 1 hour.

3. Preheat the oven to 180°C/gas mark 4. Line three large baking trays with baking parchment.

4. Roll out the gingerbread dough on a large sheet of greaseproof paper to 5mm thickness. Using the cutter(s) of your choice, cut out the dough (re-rolling any scraps) and then use a palette knife to transfer them to the baking trays. Leave space between each one for them to spread a little. Cut out small rounds or other shapes in the centre of each biscuit, making sure you leave a good border around the edge.

5. Using the end of a drinking straw, press it into the top of each biscuit where you would like to thread a ribbon or raffia to hang it, then twist the straw and pull away to remove a tiny circle of dough. Alternatively, use a skewer to make the holes. Place the baking trays in the freezer for 10 minutes.

6. Remove from the freezer, then fill the hole in the centre of each biscuit (not the hole for the ribbon!) with a small pile of crushed boiled sweets

7. Bake for 6–10 minutes, depending on size, until golden-brown at the edges Once cooked, check the hanging holes are still large enough to thread ribbon through; if not, use a skewer or the tip of a sharp knife to increase the size slightly.

8. Leave the biscuits to cool on the baking trays until the boiled sweets have hardened, then transfer them to a wire rack to cool completely. Once cold (after about 2 hours), tie each biscuit with rainbow-coloured ribbons or raffia, ready to hang.

ROCKY ROAD

SERVES 16   PREP TIME: 15 MINUTES   COOK TIME: 5-10 MINUTES

The king of all rocky road! Intensely chocolatey and jam-packed with treats – this is definitely one to be enjoyed on a special occasion.

250g unsalted butter, plus extra for greasing
600g dark chocolate (minimum 70% cocoa solids), roughly chopped
3 tablespoons golden syrup
150g plain sandwich biscuits
80g pink wafer biscuits, halved
150g coloured marshmallows
100g honeycomb, broken into pieces
140g Crispie M&M's
1 teaspoon rainbow sprinkles/nonpareils

1. Grease and line a 20cm square cake tin with baking parchment. Melt the butter, chocolate and syrup together in a medium, heavy-based pan over a low heat, stirring until smooth and combined. Set aside to cool a little.

2. Pour a 1cm layer of the chocolate mixture over the base of the prepared tin. Scatter half of each of the biscuits, marshmallows, honeycomb and M&M's over the base. Pour over half of the remaining chocolate mixture, then shake the tin a little to allow the chocolate to fill the holes.

3. Make a second layer with the remaining biscuits, marshmallows, honeycomb and M&M's (reserving a few to scatter over the top), then pour over the remaining chocolate mixture. Shake the tin as before to encourage the chocolate into any holes.

4. Scatter with the reserved ingredients and then finally scatter over the rainbow sprinkles. Leave to set somewhere cool (or the fridge) for at least 4 hours, before cutting into squares, to serve.

SWAP IN YOUR FAVOURITE BISCUITS OR SWEETS, JUST STICK TO THE QUANTITIES ABOVE SO IT SETS AND HOLDS TOGETHER WELL.

MULTICOLOURED MACAROONS

MAKES 28   PREP TIME: 25 MINUTES, PLUS 30 MINUTES RESTING AND COOLING   COOK TIME: 10-12 MINUTES

Who can resist a macaroon, especially when they come in a colour medley!

250g ground almonds
350g icing sugar
6 large egg whites
170g caster sugar
75g salted butter, softened
food colouring pastes (purple,
 blue, green, yellow, orange
 and pink)
2 tablespoons rainbow sprinkles/
 nonpareils

FOR THE BUTTERCREAM

225g salted butter, softened
150g icing sugar
food colouring pastes (see above)

YOU WILL NEED

11 disposable piping bags

MACAROONS ARE VERY VULNERABLE TO HUMIDITY AND SMELLS, SO STORE THE SANDWICHED PAIRS IN AN AIRTIGHT CONTAINER IN THE FRIDGE FOR UP TO 7 DAYS. STACK THEM CAREFULLY, WITH GREASEPROOF PAPER BETWEEN EACH LAYER.

1. Line three baking trays with baking parchment. Whizz the ground almonds and icing sugar together in a food-processor until fine. Set aside.

2. Using an electric hand whisk, whisk the egg whites in a large, grease-free bowl until soft peaks form, then gradually whisk in the caster sugar until glossy. Sift the almond mixture over the egg whites and gently fold through with a large metal spoon.

3. Divide the mixture between seven bowls, then add a little food colouring paste to six of the bowls, gently folding it through evenly, then fold the rainbow sprinkles through the remaining bowl. Be very gentle when folding, so the mixtures don't become too loose or runny and therefore difficult to pipe.

4. Spoon one portion of coloured mixture into a piping bag and snip off the tip to make a 1cm opening. Pipe 2.5cm rounds onto the baking trays (each batch of mixture will make about 8 macaroons). Repeat with the remaining coloured mixtures and the sprinkles mixture, using a fresh piping bag each time.

5. Tap the baking trays twice on the work surface to flatten out the macaroons and to dislodge any air bubbles. If any peaks are left, lightly wet a finger and gently dab the peak flat. Set aside to rest for 30 minutes, or until the macaroons have formed a skin on the surface when you lightly touch them.

6. Meanwhile, preheat the oven to 150°C/gas mark 2. Bake the macaroons for 10-12 minutes, then leave then to cool.

7. For the buttercream, beat the butter and icing sugar together in a small bowl until light and fluffy. Divide between four bowls and add a little food colouring paste to each portion. Spoon each into a separate piping bag, then snip off the tip of each bag to make a 1cm opening. Pipe some buttercream onto the bases of an alternate colour macaroon, then sandwich them together with a different coloured macaroon on top.

FLOWER BISCUITS

MAKES 28   PREP TIME: 45 MINUTES, PLUS CHILLING AND COOLING   COOK TIME: 10-12 MINUTES

Get your piping bags at the ready! These bright flower biscuits are super simple to make and elegant too, providing a perfect gift for Mother's Day.

200g unsalted butter, softened
200g caster sugar
zest of 1 orange
1 large egg, lightly beaten
400g plain flour, plus extra
   for dusting

FOR THE BUTTERCREAM

250g unsalted butter, softened
500g icing sugar, sifted
food colouring pastes (blue, green,
   yellow, orange and pink)

YOU WILL NEED

7cm round cookie cutter
5 disposable piping bags
2cm closed star nozzle

1. Using an electric hand whisk, beat the butter, caster sugar and orange zest together in a medium bowl until just combined and becoming creamy (don't overwork, otherwise the cookies will spread during baking). Add the egg and beat until combined. Sift in the flour and stir gently until the mixture comes together to form a dough. Shape into a ball, then cut in half and wrap each portion in clingfilm. Chill in the fridge for 1 hour.

2. Line two or three large baking trays with baking parchment, then set aside. On a lightly floured surface, roll out the dough to 5mm thickness. Using the cookie cutter, cut out 28 cookies, then transfer them to the prepared baking trays. Chill in the fridge again for 30 minutes, or speed things up by chilling them in the freezer for 15 minutes.

3. Meanwhile, preheat the oven to 180°C/gas mark 4. Remove the cookies from the fridge and bake for 10–12 minutes until golden-brown at the edges. Cool for 5 minutes on the baking trays, then transfer to a wire rack and leave to cool completely.

4. For the buttercream, beat the butter and icing sugar together in a bowl until light and fluffy. Divide between five smaller bowls and stir a little food colouring paste into each portion.

5. Spoon one of the icings into a piping bag fitted with the nozzle and pipe swirls from the centre working outwards, gradually tapering them off so they look like roses. Wash the nozzle and insert into a clean piping bag then fill with another coloured icing to continue piping flowers onto the biscuits. Repeat this process with the remaining icings. Leave to set, uncovered, in a cool place for 2–3 hours.

COOKIE CAKE

SERVES 10   PREP TIME: 20 MINUTES, PLUS COOLING   COOK TIME: 25-30 MINUTES

Looking for something a little different to celebrate someone's birthday?
This soft giant cookie cake studded with a rainbow of chocolates is bound
to put a smile on anybody's face.

125g unsalted butter, softened, plus extra for greasing

75g soft light brown sugar

75g granulated sugar

1 medium egg

1 teaspoon vanilla extract

225g plain flour, plus extra for dusting

½ teaspoon baking powder

1 teaspoon bicarbonate of soda

½ teaspoon fine salt

100g hazelnuts or macadamia nuts, roughly chopped

125g dark chocolate (minimum 70% cocoa solids), roughly chopped

180g peanut M&M's or other flavoured M&M's

1. Preheat the oven to 180°C/gas mark 4. Grease a 22cm loose-based cake tin, then lightly dust with flour to coat.

2. Using an electric hand whisk, beat the butter and sugars together in a medium bowl until light and fluffy. Add the egg and vanilla extract and beat again to combine. Sift in the flour, baking powder, bicarbonate of soda and salt, then fold into the mixture until just combined.

3. Stir through three-quarters of each of the nuts, chocolate chunks and M&M's, then press the mixture evenly into the prepared tin. Scatter with the remaining nuts, chocolate and M&M's and press into the dough slightly.

4. Bake for 25-30 minutes until golden and puffed. Cover with foil after 15 minutes if it is beginning to brown too quickly. Leave to cool completely in the tin before removing and slicing into wedges to serve.

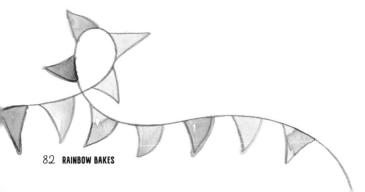

SWEETS & DESSERTS

RAINBOW FUDGE

MAKES 60 PIECES   PREP TIME: 30 MINUTES, PLUS FREEZING AND CHILLING   COOK TIME: 5-10 MINUTES

This is the simplest cheat's fudge you will ever make — there is no boiling involved, so it is safe and fun to make with children.

vegetable or sunflower oil,
   for greasing
450g good-quality white chocolate
   (minimum 30% cocoa solids),
   roughly chopped
397g can condensed milk
30g salted butter
½ teaspoon orange extract
food colouring pastes (purple, blue,
   green, yellow, orange and red)

1. Lightly grease a 16 x 10 x 8cm loaf tin with a little oil and line with clingfilm.

2. Place the white chocolate, condensed milk and butter in a medium, heavy-based saucepan and set it over a low-medium heat. Stir gently until melted, smooth and combined, then stir in the orange extract.

3. Divide between six bowls and stir a little food colouring paste into each portion until well combined.

4. Pour the purple mixture into the lined loaf tin and freeze for 15 minutes. Meanwhile, cover the remaining bowls with clingfilm. Repeat this process with the blue, green, yellow, orange and red mixtures, pouring each mixture over the previous layer and freezing each layer as above. Cover with clingfilm and leave to set overnight in the fridge until firm.

5. Turn out onto a chopping board, peel off the clingfilm and cut the fudge into 20 even slices, then cut each slice into three pieces. Store in an airtight container in the fridge to keep the fudge nice and firm.

PACKED INTO AN AIRTIGHT CONTAINER (WITH BAKING PARCHMENT BETWEEN EACH LAYER) AND STORED IN THE FRIDGE, THIS FUDGE WILL KEEP WELL FOR UP TO 2 WEEKS.

RAINBOW UNICORN BALLS

MAKES 28   PREP TIME: 40 MINUTES, PLUS COOLING, FREEZING, SETTING AND CHILLING   COOK TIME: 15 MINUTES

These truffles are great as gifts and for sharing with friends.

175ml whipping cream

pinch of salt

75g granulated sugar

125g unsalted butter, softened

2 tablespoons rainbow sprinkles/
nonpareils

TO COAT AND DECORATE

150g good-quality dark chocolate
(minimum 70% cocoa solids),
roughly chopped

150g good-quality white chocolate
(minimum 30% cocoa solids),
roughly chopped

2 teaspoons peanut, almond or
walnut oil

3 tablespoons rainbow sprinkles/
nonpareils

YOU WILL NEED

large piping bag fitted with a large
round nozzle

● ● ● ● ● ● ● ● ● ● ● ● ● ● ●

**FOR ADDED FLAVOUR, USE FLAVOURED
CHOCOLATE OR STIR IN 1 TABLESPOON
OF YOUR FAVOURITE LIQUEUR OR 1
TEASPOON OF ORANGE OR PEPPERMINT
EXTRACT WHEN YOU STIR THE SUGAR
IN TO THE MIXTURE IN STEP 1.**

● ● ● ● ● ● ● ● ● ● ● ● ● ● ●

1. Line two baking trays with baking parchment and set aside.
Pour the whipping cream into a saucepan and add the salt.
Set over a low heat and bring to just below boiling point.
Remove from the heat and stir in the sugar until dissolved.
Set aside to cool to 20°C (room temperature).

2. Using an electric hand whisk, beat the butter in a medium
bowl until light and fluffy. Gradually pour in the cream mixture,
beating continuously until smooth and combined. (If the
mixture curdles, it is too cold, but you can rescue it by gently
heating the bowl in a bain-marie until it re-emulsifies. If your
mixture is too runny, place the bowl in a bowl of iced water and
whisk until it thickens.) Add the sprinkles and stir to combine.

3. Spoon the truffle mixture into the piping bag and then pipe
neat walnut-sized rounds onto your prepared baking trays.
Transfer the trays to the freezer and leave to set for 1 hour.

4. Meanwhile, place each type of chocolate in a separate
heatproof bowl and add 1 teaspoon of the oil to each. Set one
bowl over a pan of barely simmering water, making sure the
base of the bowl doesn't touch the water, and leave for about 5
minutes until the chocolate is melted and smooth, stirring once
or twice. Repeat with the other bowl of chocolate. Remove
from the heat and set aside to cool to 40°C (about hand-hot).

5. Once the truffle centres are ready, dip them, one at a time,
into the melted chocolates (dipping half of them into the dark
chocolate and the remainder into the white chocolate). Lift
each truffle out by scooping it up with a fork and allowing the
excess chocolate to dribble off back into the bowl. Place the
truffles back on the lined baking trays and then scatter with the
sprinkles. Place in the fridge for 1 hour to set before serving.
These truffles will keep well the fridge, in an airtight container
(with baking parchment between each layer) for two weeks.

FRUIT JELLIES

**MAKES 30 JELLIES OF YOUR CHOSEN FLAVOUR   PREP TIME: 30 MINUTES, PLUS COOLING AND SETTING
COOK TIME: 15–25 MINUTES**

Bursting with natural fruits, these jellies are packed with tangy flavour.

vegetable oil, for greasing

400–500g prepared fruit for one
flavour (see flavours, below)

300g caster sugar

2 tablespoons lemon juice

3 tablespoons apple-based
liquid pectin

150g granulated sugar

FOR PINEAPPLE FLAVOUR

400g chopped
pineapple flesh, plus a little
yellow food colouring paste

FOR BLACKBERRY FLAVOUR

400g blackberries

FOR STRAWBERRY FLAVOUR

400g hulled and
quartered strawberries

FOR MANDARIN FLAVOUR

400g drained, canned
mandarin segments

FOR KIWI FLAVOUR

500g peeled and chopped
kiwi fruit, plus a little green
food colouring paste

YOU WILL NEED

sugar thermometer

1. Lightly grease a 16 x 10 x 8cm loaf tin and line with clingfilm, making sure it goes right up the sides and into the corners of the tin.

2. Whizz your chosen fruit in a small blender until smooth. Press through a fine sieve to remove any pith or seeds. Transfer the fruit purée (which will now be about 300g) to a heavy-based saucepan and add the caster sugar. Place over a low heat and stir gently until the sugar has dissolved.

3. Gradually increase the heat, stirring constantly so the mixture doesn't catch and burn, until it reaches 107°C on a sugar thermometer. This will take between 10–20 minutes (be careful as some fruits have a higher pectin content than others, so some will reach the temperature and thicken more quickly).

4. Add the lemon juice and pectin and stir to combine, then reheat until the mixture again reaches a temperature of 107°C (setting point) and it is thick and like a soft jam. (To test this, get a small bowl of cold chilled water and drop half a teaspoon of the mixture into it. It should hold together and set in a small ball. If not, return the pan to the heat and continue to cook for a further few minutes before testing again.) Once the mixture has reached setting point, stir in the food colouring paste (if using), then pour into the lined tin and leave to cool. Cover with clingfilm and leave to set somewhere cool or in the fridge overnight.

5. Pour the granulated sugar into a baking tray. Turn the fruit jelly block out onto the sugar and gently peel off the clingfilm. Run a large sharp knife under a hot tap then wipe dry and cut the jelly block into cubes, then gently turn them in the sugar to coat. Leave to set, uncovered, for 1 hour before serving. Packed into an airtight container, with baking parchment between each layer, they will keep in a cool, dry place for up to 3 weeks.

RAINBOW BARK

SERVES 8   PREP TIME: 15 MINUTES, PLUS SETTING AND CHILLING   COOK TIME: 10 MINUTES

This beautiful natural rainbow, made from mixed dried fruits and nuts, makes a simple chocolate treat something much more special. Great for Father's Day and so simple that the kids can make it by themselves.

500g dark chocolate (minimum 70% cocoa solids), roughly chopped

50g white chocolate (minimum 30% cocoa solids), roughly chopped

10g whole freeze-dried raspberries

50g dried banana chips

10g dried mango, cut into strips

10g pistachios, roughly chopped

10g dried coconut flakes

1. Line a 20 x 30cm Swiss roll tin with baking parchment and set aside.

2. Place each chocolate in a separate heatproof bowl. Set one bowl over a pan of barely simmering water, making sure the base of the bowl doesn't touch the water, and leave for about 5 minutes until the chocolate is melted and smooth, stirring once or twice. Repeat with the other bowl of chocolate. Remove from the heat.

3. Pour the melted dark chocolate into the prepared tin and leave to cool slightly at room temperature, about 5 minutes. Place spoonfuls of the melted white chocolate randomly over the dark chocolate and then use a skewer or the tip of a sharp knife to marble the chocolates together.

4. Leave again at room temperature for 5–10 minutes until set slightly but still soft, then scatter over the raspberries, banana, mango, pistachios and coconut flakes.

5. Transfer to the fridge and leave to set hard for 2 hours. Once set, turn out of the tin and break up roughly into shards. Stored in an airtight container, somewhere cool, this bark will keep well for up to 2 weeks.

SCATTER WITH ANY OF YOUR FAVOURITE DRIED FRUITS AND NUTS. YOU CAN EVEN FINISH OFF WITH A SPRINKLE OF SEA SALT OR CHILLI FLAKES FOR A LITTLE KICK!

RAINBOW MERINGUES

MAKES 40   PREP TIME: 30 MINUTES   COOK TIME: 30-35 MINUTES

Soft, chewy and small enough to pop a few in your mouth without any one seeing! These pretty little meringues make the perfect gift.

2 medium egg whites (about 60g)
about 120g caster sugar (double
   the weight of the egg whites)
½ teaspoon vanilla extract
¼ teaspoon fine salt
food colouring pastes (purple, blue,
   green, yellow, orange and pink)

YOU WILL NEED

long fine paintbrush
large disposable piping bag fitted
   with a 1cm round nozzle

● ● ● ● ● ● ● ● ● ● ● ● ● ● ● ● ●

**USE A PAPER TOWEL AND A LITTLE
WHITE WINE VINEGAR TO CLEAN YOUR
BOWL AND WHISK ATTACHMENTS
BEFORE WHISKING THE EGG WHITES
TO ENSURE EVERYTHING IS GREASE
FREE, ALLOWING THE EGG WHITES
TO WHISK UP WELL.**

● ● ● ● ● ● ● ● ● ● ● ● ● ● ● ● ●

1. Preheat the oven to 120°C/gas ½. Line two or three baking trays with baking parchment.

2. Using an electric hand whisk, whisk the egg whites in a medium, grease-free bowl, starting with a low speed and gradually increasing it to high, until stiff peaks form. Begin to add the sugar, a tablespoon at a time, whisking well after each addition, until all the sugar is incorporated. Whisk the mixture for a further 5 minutes to completely dissolve all the sugar. You can check this by rubbing a little meringue mixture between your fingers to make sure no grains remain. If it's still grainy, continue to whisk a little more.

3. Once the meringue is smooth and glossy, whisk in the vanilla extract and salt.

4. Take the piping bag and turn the top down about halfway. Using the paintbrush, draw lines of food colouring paste on the inside of the bag all the way up from the nozzle end to the wider open top of the bag. For pastel shades use a thin line of paste, and for more intense colours use a thicker line of paste. Remember to clean the brush between applying each colour.

5. Once you have drawn all the coloured lines on the inside of the piping bag, carefully add spoonfuls of meringue to the bag, starting as low down in the bag as you can. Make sure the bag doesn't collapse and spread the colours. Gently pull the sides of the bag back up and twist the top to secure. (You can place the piping bag in a measuring jug and fold the top of the bag down over the sides of the jug, then add the colours and meringue. This keeps the piping bag in place and avoids any slippages.)

6. Pipe small teardrops onto the prepared baking trays, leaving about 5cm between each one. Bake for 30–35 minutes. When the meringues are ready, they will pull off the paper easily – if they don't, pop them back in for a few more minutes until they are ready. Set aside to cool on the baking trays for 1 hour, then peel off the paper. Serve or store. Stored in an airtight container (with baking parchment between each layer), these meringues will keep well, in a cool, dry place, for up to 2 weeks.

FRUIT ROLLS

MAKES 10 ROLLS OF YOUR CHOSEN FLAVOUR   PREP TIME: 15 MINUTES   COOK TIME: 8-10 HOURS

These healthy snacks are a real hit with kids and make a great swap for sweets in lunch boxes.

FOR THE RASPBERRY AND ROSEWATER FLAVOUR

200g raspberries
¼ teaspoon rosewater
1 tablespoon caster sugar or honey

FOR THE BLACKBERRY, LIME AND MINT FLAVOUR

200g blackberries
juice of ½ lime
10 mint leaves
1 tablespoon caster sugar or honey

FOR THE PLUM AND VANILLA FLAVOUR

200g (prepared weight) plums,
   stoned and chopped
¼ teaspoon vanilla extract
1 tablespoon caster sugar or honey

FOR THE MANGO AND LIME FLAVOUR

200g (prepared weight) fresh
   mango, peeled, stoned
   and chopped
juice of ½ lime
1 tablespoon caster sugar or honey

FOR THE STRAWBERRY FLAVOUR

200g (prepared weight)
   strawberries, hulled and halved
1 tablespoon caster sugar or honey

1. Preheat the oven to 60°C. If you use an electric fan oven, then the fruit dries out much more quickly and can cause the fruit rolls to crack, and gas ovens do not have a temperature this low, so in these cases, preheat the oven to its lowest temperature and check the fruit rolls after just half the cooking time given below. Line a baking tray, about 25 x 35cm, with baking parchment.

2. Choose your flavour, then wash and prepare the fruit. Put the fruit in a blender with the other flavourings listed for each one (if applicable), along with the sugar or honey. Whizz to a smooth purée. Pour the mixture into the lined baking tray and tilt the tin to spread the purée out evenly.

3. Bake for 8-10 hours or overnight until dry to touch. Remove from the oven and leave to cool completely on the baking tray. Once cold, peel off the lining paper, then cut the fruit mixture into strips and roll up. Stored in an airtight container (with baking parchment between each layer), these fruit rolls will keep well in a cool, dry place for up to 3 weeks.

● ●

YOU CAN BAKE UP TO THREE BATCHES OF FRUIT ROLLS AT THE SAME TIME – MAKE ONE BATCH AFTER THE OTHER AND POP EACH ONE INTO THE OVEN AS YOU GO. ABOUT HALFWAY THROUGH, SWAP THE POSITION OF THE TRAYS AROUND.

IF YOU WANT TO LIVEN UP THE COLOUR OF THE FRUIT PURÉES, SIMPLY STIR A LITTLE FOOD COLOURING PASTE INTO THE PURÉE BEFORE POURING IT INTO THE TIN TO BAKE.

● ●

RAINBOW CREPE CAKE WITH WHITE CHOCOLATE GANACHE

SERVES 12   PREP TIME: 30 MINUTES, PLUS CHILLING AND COOLING   COOK TIME: 1¼ HOURS

For those who just aren't into cake (I know, crazy right?!) or are just looking for something a little bit different, this impressive crepe tower will hit the spot perfectly.

FOR THE WHIPPED CHOCOLATE GANACHE

750ml double cream
450g white chocolate (minimum 30% cocoa solids), finely chopped

FOR THE CREPES

1.4 litres whole milk
175g unsalted butter, plus extra for greasing
12 large eggs
400g plain flour
120g caster sugar
½ teaspoon salt
zest of 2 oranges
food colouring pastes (purple, blue, green, yellow, orange and red)
1 tablespoon icing sugar, to dust
1 tablespoon edible gold stars

1. First make the whipped chocolate ganache. Pour the cream into a medium saucepan over a low heat and bring to just below boiling point. Remove from the heat, add the chopped chocolate and leave to melt for 1 minute, then stir gently until smooth and combined. Pour into a bowl and leave to cool, then cover and chill in the fridge for at least 2 hours until firm. Once chilled, beat with an electric hand whisk until soft peaks form.

2. Once the ganache is chilling, you can make the crepes. Heat the milk in a medium, heavy-based saucepan until small bubbles appear at the edges. Meanwhile, melt the butter in a separate pan. Set both aside and leave to cool slightly.

3. Using a stand mixer with a whisk attachment, or an electric hand whisk, whisk the eggs, flour, caster sugar, salt and orange zest together until combined. Reduce to a low speed and then gradually add the butter and milk until incorporated.

4. Divide the batter between six bowls and stir a little food colouring paste into each portion.

5. Heat two large (22cm diameter) frying pans over a low-medium heat and grease each one with a little butter. Pour a few tablespoons of the first coloured batter into each pan and swirl each to coat the pan evenly. Cook for 1–2 minutes until the edges begin to brown, then flip the crepes and cook for an additional 1–1½ minutes. Remove the cooked crepes to a large plate and place a sheet of greaseproof paper in-between each one. Repeat (greasing the pans between each use) until all the

coloured batters are used up, stacking the crepes as you go. Set the cooked crepes aside and leave to cool completely.

6. To assemble, stack the coloured crepes on top of each other, spreading a thin layer of the whipped chocolate ganache between each one, working your way through the colours of the rainbow as you stack. Once assembled, chill the crepe cake in the fridge for 2 hours, then dust with icing sugar and edible gold stars just before serving. Cut into wedges to serve.

MARBLED MARSHMALLOWS

**MAKES 48 MARSHMALLOWS OF YOUR 2 CHOSEN FLAVOURS   PREP TIME: 50 MINUTES, PLUS COOLING AND SETTING
COOK TIME: 15 MINUTES**

You haven't experienced a marshmallow until you have tried a home-made one. Billowy and white, they are the perfect sweet treat to flavour and colour, to create a rainbow of irresistible, lighter-than-air marshmallows.

1 teaspoon sunflower oil

30g icing sugar

30g cornflour

16g (about 8–9 sheets) leaf gelatine

500g granulated sugar

1 tablespoon glucose syrup

2 large egg whites

food colouring pastes of your choice to match the flavourings (optional)

FOR THE FLAVOURS

Pineapple and lime

400g chopped pineapple flesh

1 tablespoon granulated sugar

zest and juice of ½ lime

Blackberry and mint

350g blackberries

1 tablespoon granulated sugar

juice of ½ lemon

sprig of fresh mint, leaves picked and finely chopped

Raspberry

350g raspberries

1 tablespoon granulated sugar

juice of ½ lemon

Pistachio

75g pistachios, roughly chopped

green food colouring paste

1. Choose two flavours and place the ingredients for each (except with the pistachio one) into separate medium, heavy-based saucepans and set over a medium heat. Bring to the boil, then simmer for 5–10 minutes, stirring frequently, until thick and jammy. Cool slightly, then press the mixture through a fine sieve to remove any seeds and excess pulp. Set aside to cool slightly.

2. Grease a 20 x 30cm rectangle cake tin with the sunflower oil. Sift the icing sugar and cornflour together in a small bowl, then dust the tin with the mixture, tapping it over the base and up the sides to create an even coating. Tap out any excess into a small bowl, then cover and reserve.

3. Place the gelatine leaves in a shallow bowl of cold water and set aside.

4. Place the granulated sugar, glucose syrup and 250ml of cold water in a medium, heavy-based saucepan over a low heat. Stir frequently until the sugar has dissolved, then insert a sugar thermometer and increase the heat. Bring the sugar syrup up to a temperature of 128°C, without stirring, then remove from the heat.

5. Using an electric hand whisk, whisk the egg whites in a large, grease-free bowl until stiff peaks form. Once the sugar syrup is ready, continue whisking the egg whites on a low speed whilst carefully pouring the hot sugar syrup down the inside edge of the bowl.

6. Gently squeeze the excess liquid out of the soaked gelatine, then add the gelatine to the egg white mixture. Gradually increase the whisking speed to high, continuing until the

mixture is thick and holds its shape on the whisk when you lift it out. It will have doubled in size.

7. Transfer half of the egg white mixture into another bowl, then fold your two cooled flavoured pulps through one portion each to gently marble. At this point you can add a little food colouring paste if you want a more vibrant colour. If you are making the pistachio flavour, just fold the nuts through the egg white mixture now along with a little green food colouring paste.

8. Tilting the prepared tin, spoon one of the mixtures into one side of the tin, then place the tin flat and quickly spoon in the other flavour so the two flavours meet in the middle. Smooth the surface with a wet spatula. Tightly cover the tin with clingfilm, ensuring the clingfilm doesn't touch the marshmallow mixture, then set aside somewhere cool (but not the fridge) for at least 4 hours or overnight.

9. Once set, dust a chopping board with the reserved icing sugar and cornflour mixture. Pass a knife all around the edge of the marshmallow to loosen it and turn out onto the board. Cut into squares with a wet sharp knife, cleaning the knife after every few slices. Roll each square in the icing sugar and cornflour mixture to coat. Serve or store.

FRUIT SORBET ICE CREAM CAKE

SERVES 16 PREP TIME: 1-1¼ HOURS, PLUS FREEZING

This is soon to be your new favourite dessert! Treat friends to a slice
of wonderful, tasty rainbow flavours and colours.

500ml strawberry sorbet
500ml mango sorbet
500ml blueberry frozen yogurt
500ml lemon sorbet
500ml raspberry sorbet
500ml pistachio ice cream

FOR THE WHIPPED CREAM ICING

400ml whipping cream
50g icing sugar, sifted
½ teaspoon vanilla extract

TO DECORATE

250g mixed frozen fruit

1. Line a 23cm loose-based round cake tin with two layers of
   clingfilm. Remove the first sorbet from the freezer and remove
   all the packaging. Cut the sorbet into slices and press into the
   lined tin with the back of a large spoon, spreading it level.
   Place in the freezer and leave for 1½-2 hours, or until set hard.

2. Repeat with the next sorbet, pressing the slices in an even layer
   over the first sorbet layer, then freeze again, as above. Continue
   in the same way with the remaining sorbets, frozen yogurt and
   ice cream, freezing each layer as before (you can choose if you
   would like the layers to be in the order of a traditional rainbow
   or if you prefer a more random theme to your coloured layers).

3. Once they are all used up and layered on top of each other,
   cover the whole tin with clingfilm and freeze for several hours
   or overnight until firm (the dessert can now stay in the freezer
   until you are ready to serve).

4. When you are ready to serve the sorbet cake, remove it
   from the freezer, uncover and carefully release it from the
   tin, peeling off the clingfilm. Place it on a serving plate
   and return to the freezer for 30 minutes to set the surface.

5. Meanwhile, for the whipped cream icing, using an electric
   hand mixer, whip the cream in a medium bowl until soft peaks
   form, then whisk in the icing sugar and vanilla extract until
   combined. Immediately spread the icing over the frozen cake
   with a palette knife. Return the cake to the freezer for a further
   15 minutes to firm up, then remove and scatter with the frozen
   fruit. Cut into wedges to serve.

MARBLED CHEESECAKE

SERVES 16 PREP TIME: 40 MINUTES, PLUS COOLING AND CHILLING COOK TIME: 1 HOUR 40 MINUTES

What better way to end a meal than with this rainbow-swirled, creamy
vanilla cheesecake with a crunchy ginger biscuit base?

½ teaspoon vegetable oil
350g ginger biscuits
125g unsalted butter, melted
1kg full-fat cream cheese, at
  room temperature
250g granulated sugar
4 large eggs, lightly beaten
240ml soured cream
1 teaspoon vanilla extract
2 tablespoons cornflour
food colouring pastes (blue, green,
  orange and pink)

1. Preheat the oven to 160°C/gas mark 3. Pour some water into
   a large, shallow roasting tin and place it in the bottom of the
   oven. Grease a 23cm springform tin with the vegetable oil
   and line the base with baking parchment.

2. Whizz the biscuits in a food-processor until you have fine
   crumbs. Transfer to a bowl and stir through the melted butter.
   Press into the base and up the sides of the tin using the back
   of a spoon to flatten it evenly. Bake for 10 minutes, then leave
   to cool completely.

3. Reduce the oven temperature to 120°C/gas mark ½. Using an
   electric hand whisk, beat the cream cheese and sugar together
   in a large bowl until light and fluffy. Lightly beat in the eggs,
   a little at a time, until combined. Beat in the soured cream,
   vanilla extract and cornflour until smooth and combined.

4. Place one-third of the mixture in a bowl, then divide the
   remaining mixture between four bowls. Stir a little food
   colouring paste into each of the portions until well combined.
   Using a large spoon, alternately place the plain and coloured
   mixtures over the biscuit base. Use the tip of a sharp knife to
   gently swirl the colours together, creating a marbled effect.

5. Bake for 1½ hours, or until the filling is set but still jiggles
   slightly in the centre when the tin is gently nudged. Turn the
   oven off and leave the cheesecake to cool completely inside
   before taking it out. Chill in the fridge for at least 3–4 hours or
   overnight before removing from the tin and serving in slices.

**YOU CAN LAYER UP THE
CHEESECAKE BATTER IN THE
TIN AS AN ALTERNATIVE TO
MARBLING IF YOU WISH.**

RAINBOW OF FRUIT TART

SERVES 10   PREP TIME: 40 MINUTES, PLUS CHILLING AND COOLING   COOK TIME: 20 MINUTES

Liven up your dessert with a natural burst of colour. This beautiful tart is so easy to assemble and is bound to impress.

FOR THE PASTRY

85g unsalted butter, softened
60g caster sugar
3 large egg yolks
200g plain flour, plus extra
  for dusting

FOR THE TOPPING

120ml double cream
120g mascarpone cheese
300g natural Greek yogurt
50g icing sugar, sifted
1 teaspoon vanilla extract
600g prepared and washed mixed
  fresh fruit (such as papaya,
  mango, kiwi, passion fruit,
  clementine segments, whole
  berries and grapes), sliced or
  left whole as you wish
zest of 1 lime

YOU WILL NEED

baking beans or raw rice

1. Using an electric hand whisk, beat the butter and sugar together in a medium bowl until creamy, then beat in the egg yolks, one at a time, until combined. Sift over the flour and fold in until the mixture comes together to form a dough.

2. Tip the dough onto a lightly floured surface and knead briefly until smooth. Roll into a ball, then press gently into a disc, wrap in clingfilm and chill in the fridge for 30 minutes.

3. Preheat the oven to 200°C/gas mark 6. Roll out the pastry on a lightly floured surface to a 45 x 22cm rectangle, then use it to line a 35 x 12cm fluted rectangular tart tin (the pastry will hang over the edges of the tin, which is correct – you'll trim these to neaten later). Place on a baking tray, then prick the base of the tart all over with a fork, line with greaseproof paper and fill with baking beans or raw rice.

4. Bake for 15 minutes. Remove the paper and baking beans or rice and bake for a further 5 minutes. Remove from the oven and leave to cool completely on a wire rack. Trim off the excess pastry with a sharp knife to neaten the edges, then carefully remove from the tin and place the tart case on a serving plate.

5. Whip the cream in a bowl until soft peaks form, then whisk in the mascarpone, yogurt, icing sugar and vanilla extract. Spoon the cream mixture into the cold tart case, spreading it out with the back of a spoon and creating a few peaks.

6. Arrange the mixed fruit over the cream mixture, then scatter with the lime zest to decorate. Serve immediately.

INDEX

THANK YOUS

First, thank you to any one who has bought one of my books and has come back for more! Baking is such a passion of mine and I love to share my recipes with others who are looking for a bit of fun and inspiration in the kitchen.

To my creative rainbow book team! It is so inspiring to work with a group of people who constantly surprise you with new wonderful ideas of how to squeeze more colour or a little joke onto a page. I've said it before but it really is true – though our jobs can be demanding they are always great fun! The delight and enthusiasm from everyone involved I believe shines through on the pages of this book and for that I am very grateful.

To Sophie, for always wanting more colour, more rainbows and more unicorns! Thank you for encouraging any kind of wackiness to help to make this book as playful as it was intended.

To Danielle, for your patience while rainbow masterpieces took time to create in the kitchen! For not being phased when increasingly more and more colourful bakes were put on set and for always managing to put together the perfect shot to show off each rainbow.

To Lauren and Lydia, for teaming up to make rainbow bakes as fun, colourful and stylish as I imagined it could be and for scouring London high and low for rainbows and unicorns galore!

To Louise, for pulling all our multi-coloured magic together and making it something wonderful. You instantly got the essence of the book and, Sarah, your tubby unicorn will live in my dreams forever!

To Millicent and Ted, for beautiful hands, strong arms and photographic skills that made our shoots breeze by.

To Amber, for washing and drying rainbow icing bowls over and over again with the knowledge that you wouldn't get to eat any of the cake!

To Bear, for the excruciating job of helping to clear up all the rainbow sprinkles that made it onto the floor.

And to Tom, this time for laughing at my rainbow icing stained feet when they poked out the end of the bed after a long, exhausting day recipe testing. For saying all the right things when sampling rainbow cake and for carrying bags and boxes back and forth to the car for the photo shoots. You are my pot of gold at the end of the rainbow.